Spy's Guide

To

Thinking

+

Strategy

by

John Braddock

**For updates on next books,
join John's email list at:**

www.spysguide.com

Contents

A Spy's Guide To Thinking

How To Think 1

What To Think About 13

How Others Think 25

How To Think About Others 42

A Spy's Guide To Strategy

Strategy 54

Games 97

The Other Side's Strategy 150

Your Strategy 192

1

How To Think

Spy gadgets are fun. Not Q's rocket cars and jetpacks. Not James Bond's remote detonators. The real world stuff. Crazy, complicated things. Fun, yes. Interesting, yes.

But if you're a spy in the field, you start to think. Do I want to bet lives – my life – on a gadget working?

You say no to a lot of gadgets. You turn down most of what they send you. When you get one that might be good, you ask questions. Does it work? Does it work in a simple way? Will it break?

Even then, you pause. You want someone else to use it first. Just to be sure. You learn the best things aren't the new things. Used things are better. Worn things. Things that have worked in the field. For fifty, sixty years, if possible. Updated, sure. But tested. Proven. If the mission fails because a gadget breaks, it's not Q at risk. It's you.

When you find something that works, it's gold. The thing does its job, you do yours. You go out and be a spy. Maybe even save the world.

The first part of this book is about thinking, but it's like a gadget. It has tools that work. In a simple way. Without breaking. Even better, the tools have been used for a long time. Updated, sure. But used successfully by people and organizations for many years.

The tools here are most useful under pressure. First, because they stop us from only reacting. They bring focus. They help us resist the takeover of the lizard brain. They remind us what sets us apart: We think.

Lastly, they've been tested in a variety of environments with a variety of people. With varying levels of complexity. Different situations, different people, different needs.

Bottom line: They work.

On that, I bet my life.

Early morning in Europe. Not the worst place. Not the

best. A weekend. Just after public transport opened. Quiet. A good time for a spy to meet a source.

I found a seat in the back of a subway car. Pulled out a phone to check for last minute communications. A guy saw me do it.

Normally, not a big deal. Lots of people dressed like me. Looked like me. Had their phones out. But the guy chose me.

"Let me see your phone," he said in the local language.

I ignored him.

"Let me see your phone," he said again.

I looked at the guy. Started thinking. Collected data.

The guy: My height. A little heavier. Wiry. Some muscle under a thin coat. Cheap shoes. Jeans. Non-native ethnicity. Aggressive posture.

He stood in the walkway. Blocked the exit. His gaze was intense. But his eyes were dancing and unfocused.

Time for some analysis.

Pretty clear that "Let me see your phone" equaled "Let me steal your phone."

More analysis needed. I started on the usual cycle of

---

questions when approached by anyone in a foreign country.

The first question was always the same: Does this guy know I'm a spy?

Thinking, in its simplest form, looks like this:

Data → Analysis→ Decision → Action

Notice the end: Action. If thinking doesn't end with action, it's useless. Taking action is why we think. If you're thinking just to think, that's useless, too.

Back up another step: Decision. We're deciding on a range of options. Simple.

Back up another: Analysis. We're sifting through the information needed to make a decision. We're judging the credibility of the information.

Its reliability. Its usefulness for the decision. And we're combining the new data with what we already know.

Then we're at the beginning: Data. We're collecting

data on the world. We're gathering what we think will be useful down the line. The information we need to analyze. To decide. To take action.

That's the chain of thinking: D-A-D-A. Getting data leads to analysis. Analysis leads to a decision. A decision leads to an action. Simple. That's how thinking works.

It's not just people who think this way. Organizations, large and small, do it, too. Instead of the process being in one head, it's spread among many. Some gather data. Some analyze it. Others make decisions. Still others take action. Some organizations do this well, some don't.

I was part of the thinking process in the largest organization of all: the U.S. government. What I did was collect data. The front end of this chain. It was secret data. Risky data. The kind of data that people can die for. People like me. Because secret data starts a process that leads to certain kinds of action. Sometimes, it leads to war.

One nation learns about a rival's weakness. Another discovers that the first is planning an invasion. A third tries to pre-empt with negotiations. A fourth takes advantage of the confusion and starts a war.

I collected secret data so the U.S. could make the right decisions. Take the right actions. Hopefully, before

---

things spun out of hand. It's the game before the game. What happens before news becomes news. That's intelligence gathering. It's collecting data to feed into a government's thinking process.

To do my job, I also did the four parts myself. Collect the data on the intelligence target. Analyze it. Make a decision on the approach. Take action to get the intelligence.

Not thinking well is dangerous. Because the spy world is risky and constantly changing. New data to collect. More analysis to do. New options to evaluate. New actions to take.

Even when you least expect it.

Does he know I'm a spy?

He had spoken to me in the local language. A good sign that he didn't know I was a spy. Or at least, an American spy.

I had to be sure. Everything I would do next depended on that answer.

Collected more data. First: What's he looking at?

My phone. Mostly my phone, anyway. A quick glance at my face just then.

The phone is what he wants. Doesn't mean he doesn't know I'm a spy. Maybe his job is to get my phone because he knows I'm a spy. If so, would he be so obvious? A follow-up: Is he here to distract me from something else?

More data needed. On the environment.

The first thing to know: Was the guy alone?

I looked around.

Sleepy faces in the seats. A young guy two rows away watching. A surprised look on his face. No tenseness in the shoulders. No readiness. No slight shift of weight. No preparation for movement. He's watching because this guy asked to see my phone. Not a normal occurrence. He's interested but not expecting to do anything. The young guy's not planning to get involved.

In front of him, an old woman in a scarf. A bag on her lap. A quick turn of the head, then back around. The Russians are famous for using old women as surveillants, but not the locals here. Doubtful she was with the security services. She's trying to avoid attention. She doesn't want to get hurt.

In front of her, two people stood up – a middle-aged woman and an older man. They moved to the far end of the car. Must have heard the guy ask for my phone. Or seen something like this before.

Conflict was coming. They didn't want any part. No one else reacted.

That didn't mean this wasn't a spy thing. Spies try to blend in. If they were sitting among the passengers, they would have just sat there. They wouldn't have moved. Not yet.

A half-second to breathe and think. Time to think through the questions again.

The still unanswered question: Was the guy alone?

Like I said before, spies like old, worn things. Proven things. Things that have stood the test of time.

The thinking process here -- Data-Analysis-Decision-Action -- dates from the 1950's. That's when a flight instructor for the U.S. Air Force took a close look at fighter pilots in a dogfight. How they think. How they act. How it all determines who wins. His name was John

Boyd.

Boyd used different words for the first two steps. Instead of Data, he used Observe. Instead of Analysis, he used Orient. But he meant the same thing. A fighter pilot collects data on an enemy pilot by observing. He analyzes by orienting himself to the enemy. He decides what to do, then acts.

When Boyd broke thinking into those steps, he discovered something interesting: Whichever pilot goes through the process quickest is the one who usually wins. He called going through the process and repeating it a loop.

Boyd's name for thinking: the OODA Loop. When you get to the end, you start the process again. You gather data on what you just did, analyze that data, and make another decision, followed by another action. Then you do it again.

Whoever "loops" most quickly in a dogfight? They usually win.

Because of Boyd's OODA Loop, the U.S. Air Force made a change. They wanted planes to let a pilot go through the OODA Loop as quickly as possible. Planes that moved as quickly as a pilot could think.

The process helped the Air Force think more clearly,

9

too. As an organization. Thinking about how a pilot thinks, they made changes. Big changes. They ditched their old way of doing things. Approached the problem differently. Came up with a new plan for more maneuverable, responsive aircraft.

The F-15 and F-16 fighter platforms were born.

Was the guy alone? Yes.

By his stance, he wasn't allowing anyone else to see what was going on. He was shielding me from the rest of the car. Isolating me. That's not something you do, if you're working with someone else. You want them to see. So they can jump in, if needed. He didn't want anyone to jump in.

He was alone.

Back to the original question: Was this a spy thing?

Couldn't be.

If it was, it wouldn't happen like this.

If the local security service wanted my phone, they would have come at me with at least a pair of guys.

Maybe more. Overwhelming force. Probably in uniform, too. To be sure no locals got involved.

And if they were going to arrest me, it wouldn't be in a subway car. It would be in the middle of some incriminating act. With the source. Probably at the safehouse I was headed to.

What about another spy service? Hostile and foreign?

No – this was too straightforward. No subtlety. Just come up and ask for my phone? No way. If a spy wanted my phone, he'd figure out a way to get it, mess with it and return it without me knowing. And, if he couldn't, he wouldn't do anything. No self-respecting spy would just ask for my phone.

Plus, dark orbs in the ceiling were recording everything. Spies, local or foreign, don't like cameras.

He's not a spy, I decided. Which means he doesn't know I'm a spy.

Question answered.

A new set of questions, then.

I reevaluated his clothes, posture and face. He wanted my phone. Why?

Still seated, I shifted my legs toward the guy. He moved closer. Almost within arm's reach. I saw

---

something new: his eyes were dilated.

It wasn't bright in the subway car, but his eyes were off. That's why his gaze was dancing and unfocused. A new hypothesis: The guy is a druggie. Because it's early morning, probably coming off last night's high. If he isn't still high. He's out of money. To get his next fix, he needs something to sell or trade. A phone is perfect. Me? I'm just the guy holding the phone.

A random mugging. Not a spy thing. Dangerous, but a different kind of dangerous. With different rules.

And a different kind of trouble. A guy high enough to be stupid. Stupid enough to start something. Something with a range of bad outcomes. Including losing my phone.

A phone that connected me to an important source.

A phone I wouldn't give up without a fight.

———————————————

2

What To Think About

I did data collection for the CIA. But the intelligence process didn't stop there. What I collected went to analysts.

The first two parts of thinking – Data and Analysis – are what intelligence agencies do. When the analysis is done, an intelligence agency generates a product. Called finished intelligence. They give that to the decision-makers.

That's thinking at an organizational level. With many brains involved. Every one responsible for a small part of the thinking process.

After the decision-makers deliberate and decide, who takes action? Maybe soldiers, in a time of war. Or diplomats, in peace. Or in the quasi-war, quasi-peace of the early 21st century, a combination. Or maybe, it's us again – the spies.

In the American system, here's how government-level thinking works:

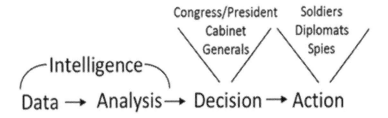

Whether spies take action or not, we always do the first part first. We go to foreign countries for secrets. We get them in the ways you see in movies. Using the occasional gadget. Then we send the secrets to the analysts.

Analysis isn't what they make movies about, but it's important. It's judging the credibility of the data. It's asking where it came from. It's understanding how close the source was to what they described. Whether the data can be trusted.

Analysis is filtering. Sifting wheat from chaff.

And analysis does something else: it combines new data with what we already know.

In my time, the big question was Iraq. Weapons of Mass Destruction (WMD) or not?

We had existing data on that. Some of it pointed to Saddam Hussein having WMD. Some of it said he didn't. Some old data said his scientists had the capability to build WMD. Some old data said they didn't.

Then there was the new data. The Niger Yellowcake. A source named Curveball. The evidence Secretary Powell presented at the UN.

Good analysis is the combination of old and new data. In a way that leads to a good decision. As in the Iraq situation, that's not easy.

Without good analysis, we can't make good decisions. Without good analysis, we can't even figure out what our options are.

Not a spy or a member of the local security service, the druggie with the dilated eyes. But still dangerous. And still wanting my phone.

Analysis done, that decision made. I turned to my next decision. What should I do?

Options were:

_____

1. Stay in my seat and let him come to me

2. Stand up and face him

3. Go on offense. Start the fight that was probably going to happen anyway.

I'm a decent athlete. Played a college sport that got rough. Had a couple concussions. Delivered some, too. I'm not afraid of contact.

But if I start a fight, will I win? Not sure. A drugged-up guy is the worst kind of opponent. Brain and body are disconnected. Pain signals don't work. He could take a beating and not feel it. Keep coming at me when he should stay down.

Worse: I wasn't sure I wanted to win. The last guy standing gets the questions. Best case scenario, the cameras would take a picture. Of me standing over a body. It would go to police stations. A bad thing for a spy in a foreign country.

Like every other spy, I just wanted to blend in.

Might not be an option.

Data collected and analysis done, I made my first big decision: my objective.

Thinking through the Data-Analysis-Decision-Action chain is an action-oriented version of another old tool you probably know: the scientific method.

The scientific method says: Develop a hypothesis, Test it and observe the results. With results in hand, decide whether your hypothesis was correct.

Albert Einstein had a hypothesis: The universe was expanding. He tested that hypothesis against the data of the day. Analyzing the data, he had a decision to make: Call his hypothesis true or false. The data said it was false, so he said it was false. The universe wasn't expanding, he decided.

Einstein later called it, "the greatest blunder of my life." But the problem wasn't with his process. It was a good process. Einstein had bad data.

When Edwin Hubble got better data and tested Einstein's hypothesis again, he found Einstein's original hypothesis was right. The universe is expanding. Hubble developed a follow-up hypothesis: The universe is expanding at a constant rate.

When more data came available, scientists tested Hubble's hypothesis. They discovered that the universe

---

is expanding, but not at a constant rate. The speed of the universe's expansion is increasing.

That's how the scientific community thinks. A hypothesis is generated. The hypothesis is tested against data. It's analyzed. A decision is made. When new data comes available, they test it again. Each loop in that process improves scientific knowledge.

You'll notice something interesting about the way scientists think: they don't start with data. They start with a hypothesis. Then they go to the data.

Good thinkers, including intelligence agencies, don't start with data, either.

The world is overflowing with data, secret and otherwise.

It has to be shrunk. That happens in the analysis process. But how do analysts decide what's important and what's not? More importantly for spies, how do we decide which secrets are worth risking lives for and which aren't?

We ask the decision-makers.

We ask them what decisions they're thinking about. What's keeping them up at night? And we ask them to look ahead. What actions do they expect to take next?

A general might say he's worried about a border war. And that a treaty might force him to intervene. For the general, the first question might be, "What's the troop strength on both sides of that border?"

A cabinet secretary might be about to sign an agreement with a rogue state. He's worried that whatever is signed won't be adhered to. For the cabinet secretary, the key question might be, "What reports from the rogue state can we trust?"

The President might be deciding whether to pursue an initiative at the UN. He's worried other nations might sabotage his effort. For the President, the key question might be, "What other nations will undermine the initiative at the UN?"

They tell the intelligence agency the issue, the options they're facing and their questions. Based on those, the analysts come up with what they call "requirements." Which are basically questions again. More open-ended than scientific hypotheses, but with the same goal: to help a decision-maker make the right decision.

Questions from the general worried about a border war might be: "How many divisions does each side have? What's their tank technology? How efficient are their supply lines?"

Questions from the cabinet secretary worried about the rogue state might be: "Do we have any independent sources of information on the rogue state's weapons? Who's the ultimate decision-maker on their side? What's the rogue state's schedule for upgrading their weapons?"

Questions from the President worried about a UN initiative might be: "Where do our allies stand on the initiative? Who's leading the opposition? What compromises will the opposition accept to work with us?"

Our analysts collect those questions. Send them to spies in the field. We get answers.

It looks like this:

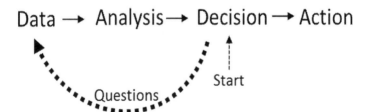

Data → Analysis → Decision → Action

Questions

Start

Intelligence agencies start with the decision. Like

scientists start with the hypothesis. That's how we know what we're looking for.

That's how we know if it's worth risking lives to get the answer.

I was the one who would take action in the subway car. I was the decision-maker. My first decision had been: Was this a spy thing or not?

Then the questions. About the guy. Whether he was alone. About others in the car. The environment. I had gathered data.

My analysis took the data and combined it with what I already knew. I knew what dilated eyes meant. I knew what a typical local looked like. And I knew what a spy approach looked like.

I had crossed the last one out. No way this was a spy thing.

Analysis done. Situation clear. On to objectives.

Primary objective today: Get intelligence from a sensitive source.

That would happen later.

Now, a druggie wants my phone. A new objective. A more immediate objective: Get past this moment without a loss. Don't let the druggie get my phone. Don't lose the game we're about to play.

Don't lose.

For spies, a typical objective. Showing a border guard a false passport? Don't lose the game. Detecting surveillance? Don't lose the game. Facing a drugged-up mugger? Don't lose the game.

Don't lose the game. Because losing this game means you don't play the next game. The next game is bigger. The next game is collecting intelligence. Finding a source that can answer the questions the decision-makers had sent.

Because the next game is bigger still: War or war averted. Lives lost or lives saved.

It didn't help to rush. Hurrying is the surest way to screw up. Screwing up slows you down. Hurrying makes the game you're trying to get past take longer.

So I took another second. Sitting in the subway car seat with a druggie blocking the way. I had decided I wouldn't go on offense. I wasn't going to start a fight, if

I didn't have to. I wasn't going to create conflict first.

That left me with a defensive strategy. And the first step in that strategy would be one of two things:

1. Stay seated

2. Stand up

I chose option 2.

I stood up. Let the druggie see I was his height. Close to his weight. Not a pushover.

I looked him in the eye.

The druggie didn't move. Just stood in the way. He wasn't backing down. Must have really needed that fix. Since he hadn't backed down, I had a different set of options.

Now there were four.

Choosing the right one depended on what I thought he would do.

When thinking about what someone else will do, it's easy to ask the wrong question first. We might ask something like, "What's the other side trying to achieve?" Or "What's their Endgame?"

Good questions for later. Not first.

The first question should always be, "What kind of game do they think we're playing?"

3

How Others Think

With billions of people, interactions between us are in the trillions every day. Individually, we interact with hundreds every day. Buying. Selling. Competing. Cooperating. Even signaling to change traffic lanes is an interaction.

Every interaction is a kind of game. Some games have winners and losers. Some games have only winners. Some have only losers.

It's impossible to think deeply about each game. There are too many. If we tried, we'd only think. Never take action. Which would be useless. Even for one person, there are too many interactions in a day to analyze each one.

Fortunately, there's a shortcut. All our interactions are only three kinds of games:

    A.   Zero-Sum

B. Positive-Sum

C. Negative-Sum

Just three.

Zero-Sum Games dominate the history books. They're conflicts. They're when one player can only gain what another player gives up.

European wars. The Germans gain Alsace-Lorraine by force, the French lose it. The Treaty of Versailles gives Alsace-Lorraine back to the French, the Germans lose it. When it comes to land, France can only gain what Germany loses, and vice-versa. When the game's finished and you add what was lost and gained by the players, it equals zero.

Politics, whether in a republic or democracy or monarchy or dictatorship, are also Zero-Sum Games. One candidate wins a seat another candidate loses. One party wins control that another party loses. One king takes power when another dies. One dictator takes over because the last is removed in a coup. Power politics are Zero-Sum Games, no matter what politicians want us to believe.

Positive-Sum Games are different. They're cooperative. They continue only as long as both sides are gaining, or expect to. Like any good marriage or alliance or business partnership, benefits to both sides is what keeps it together. When you add up the gains, the result is positive. A Positive-Sum Game.

Some Positive-Sum Games last for centuries. Like the "special relationship" between the U.S. and the U.K on diplomatic issues. Some Positive-Sum Games last for only as long as it takes to do the drive-thru at McDonald's. Whatever the context, Positive-Sum Games require exchange. They require voluntary action. Benefits to both sides.

Negative-Sum Games are rare. They're wars of attrition. Verdun. Or a labor strike. Both sides are losing. Each side hopes it's losing less than the other. As soon as one side figures it's losing too much, the Negative-Sum Game is over. Negative-Sum Games are like heavy elements that live for a short time before decaying into something else.

Understanding these three types of games is a shortcut to good thinking.[1] It helps us understand the people we're working with or against.

Best of all, the games shortcut gets us closer to the Holy Grail of thinking: predicting what others will do next.

The druggie was playing a Zero-Sum Game. He wanted my phone. Wasn't going to give me anything for it. If he wins, I lose. One winner. One loser. That was the game he wanted to play.

Conflict. No question about it. The little war we were having wasn't over anything great or noble. No land at stake. No honor. No survival of a people. No epic poems would be sung. It was just a fight over a phone.

He wanted the phone. I wanted to keep it. At the end of the game, one of us would have the phone. One wouldn't. Add up the result for us players: A Zero-Sum.

His first move in the game: Ask to "see" my phone. If I had given it to him, the game would have been over. He would have the phone. I would have lost it, because he wasn't going to give it back. Game over. Unless I escalated. Which would have been difficult for a spy trying to blend in.

But I hadn't given him my phone. So he asked again. Again, I didn't give it to him.

He had gathered some new data along the way. He had seen my reaction. Sized me up. Seen that I was going to resist. How much? He didn't know.

What kind of analysis could he do through the fog in his brain? I don't know. It was probably slow. Slow analysis leads to slow decision-making. Which means he was slow to action.

Maybe that's why I had time to stand up.

When I stood up and he saw I was his height and his size, he hadn't backed away. Maybe because he was thinking slowly. Maybe because he didn't care. Maybe I was his quickest route to a fix. Didn't matter if I was Andre the Giant. He was going to try to get my phone.

Standing face to face, I had four options:

1. Move sideways around him

2. Push him out of the way

3. Sit back down

4. Do nothing

Later a colleague suggested a fifth: Drop the phone and stomp on it. Smash it up. That way the druggie doesn't get it, and I avoided what was coming. I didn't think of that. Besides, it was an important phone. It was a link to an important source. At that point, I thought I could keep it.

With just the four options I thought of, I chose option 1.

I moved to the side.

He shifted, too. Like a dance step. Blocked my way.

Now my options were the remaining three:

1. Push him out of the way

2. Sit back down

3. Do nothing

There wasn't much more data to gather. At least, it didn't seem that way.

Then he moved his hands.

It had been only a few seconds since everything started. A few seconds since the druggie had asked for my phone. I hadn't hurried, but I'd slowed down too much. After seeing this wasn't a spy thing, I had relaxed.

I hadn't shifted to street crime defense. Druggie analysis.

I wasn't all the way inside the druggie's head.

I had looked at his face, his eyes, his build, his demeanor, his clothes.

I hadn't looked at his hands.

I hadn't looked for weapons.

When his hands moved, it was to do something to help him win. Something to help him take my phone.

I looked down to see what it was.

The first step to winning a Zero-Sum Game is to know it's coming. It's why spies work in peacetime. To be a tripwire. To give an alert when peace is about to become war. It's why the CIA was formed in the first place.

The CIA traces its origins to the Office of Strategic Services, the World War II outfit that ran covert operations behind enemy lines. The OSS story is such a part of CIA culture that my training included parachute jumps. So maybe they could drop me behind enemy lines in a war.

In fact, the CIA story is more about a peacetime failure. Before World War II, the U.S. had codebreakers but no overseas spy service. There were some attempts by the FBI, State Department, Army and Navy, but they were halfhearted.

Then came Pearl Harbor. Thousands dead. Pacific

Fleet decimated. Because the right people didn't know war was coming.

When the dust settled on World War II, it was time to say, "Never again." Could a spy service – a centralized spy service – have stopped Pearl Harbor? Maybe. Maybe not. Either way, the CIA was formed to do that. To gather data, analyze it, and pass it to the decision-makers so they would know what they needed to know. To give a heads up. Let key people know when peace was turning to war. So they could act in time.

Here's the important thing: The CIA's mission was not to centralize intelligence-gathering. The CIA would gather intelligence, yes. But so would others. The CIA's mission was to centralize the *process* of intelligence-gathering and delivery to decision-makers. It was to be sure the Data-Analysis-Decision-Action chain worked.

Over the following decades, more Zero-Sum Games came along. The Cold War. The Vietnam War. The Iraq Wars. The War on Terrorism. All conflicts that needed good intelligence. Good intelligence that would give the best possible chance of a good decision. And implementing those good decisions would, hopefully, lead to victory. Or, at least, not a loss.

When you're part of the process of preparing for war, you realize something about Zero-Sum Games. Winning isn't just about being good at conflict. In fact, being good at conflict isn't the best way to win a Zero-Sum Game.

The best way to win a Zero-Sum Game is to be good at Positive-Sum Games.

There were no Positive-Sum Games in the subway car. Not on my side, of course. I was alone.

When you're a spy, you get used to being alone. You're on planes alone. In cars alone. In hotels alone. Sometimes nice places like the Mediterranean resort where I stayed for a week waiting for someone who didn't show. Sometimes you sit for 24 hours in the freezing cold doing surveillance. You're alone and at risk. Situations where all you can do is think. And think about thinking.

Alone in the subway car: A normal situation.

There were people all around, though. Potential allies. A dozen or so.

The young man a row away was a potential ally. But he didn't want to get involved. The old lady? No – she would just get hurt, even if she wanted to help. The other two nearby had already moved.

Not that I blamed them. They didn't know me or the other guy. We could have a long-running feud. We could be about to pull guns. They didn't want to be nearby when the conflict started.

Could I have asked for help? Maybe. What would have been the druggie's reaction? Probably to accelerate what was coming.

Anyway, no good alliances available. No opportunity to increase power through partnering.

Plus, would it have been Positive-Sum? What would the others gain? Probably nothing. At least, that's what they would think. And they might get hurt. So there's a chance they would lose. Which makes everyone think twice. Any alliances on the druggie's side? No. He was alone, too, as far as I could tell.

No allies on either side. Both of us would go into this Zero-Sum Game with what we brought. I hadn't brought much. Just technology for communicating. Something else for concealment. Nothing too useful in a fight.

The druggie, on the other hand, probably played a lot of these kinds of games. He'd probably been in a lot of fights in his life. He would have been ready.

And, he was starting the conflict. So he would be prepared.

When his hands moved, I immediately thought of weapons. Cursed that I hadn't been more careful.

But it wasn't a weapon he used first.

Thinking is cheap. Action is expensive.

Collecting data takes time and resources, but modern technology makes it cheaper every day. Analyzing that data? Making sense of it? More difficult. More expensive. Making good decisions takes even more resources, usually. But the most expensive thing, nearly always, is taking action.

If you've ever been on an IT project or tried to implement a new strategy or built an addition on your house, you know how this works. You know that actually doing something costs a lot more than deciding what to do.

There's another reason action is expensive.

Something other than time and resources. It's because actions are a commitment.

Anytime in the thinking process, you can stop. You can reverse. You can move backward. You can gather more data. Do more analysis. Reconsider the decision.

Action is irreversible.

Actions, no matter how small, commit us to a particular path. Acting on Option 3 means Option 2 and Option 1 just went away. Economists call this losing the "option value." By taking one action, you lose the value of all the other options.

Costs go up as thinking moves closer to action:

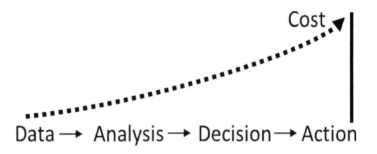

This is the right way to do it. If we do it differently, things go wrong.

Think about trying to do the D-A-D-A chain in reverse. If we spend less time analyzing than we do collecting data, we never make it through all the data. If we spend more time making decisions than we do taking action, we end up not doing much at all.

Costs go up as you get closer to action in the Data-Analysis-Decision-Action chain. That's one trend. There's another trend that goes the other way.

It has to do with how much we're working with at each step. The trend of quantity slopes down to the right. It looks like this:

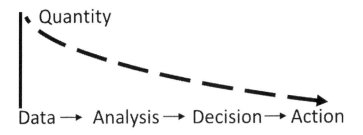

You, me, and organizations face a lot of data. Even before computers and the information revolution, we could collect more data than we could ever analyze. The weather. The environment. The people around us. There's always been more data than we could ever analyze.

Then, moving to the right, there's more analysis we can do than decisions we can make. We compare our new data to existing data. Throw out some of it. Filter it. Prioritize it. And use it for decision-making.

The decisions themselves are fewer still. There's more analysis we can do than decisions we can make.

And finally, there are more decisions we make than actions we take. Because some decisions are to stop. Some decisions are to do nothing.

In terms of quantity, actions are the fewest. Data the most.

Going to the right across the Data-Analysis-Decision-Action chain, the quantity goes down. While the cost goes up.

Put together, the two trends look like this:

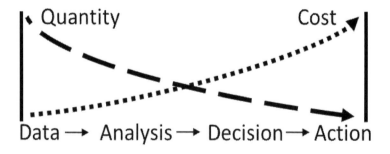

There's a tension here. That tension is tough on our thinking.

It's worse for organizations. Most groups put most of their resources into action, as they should. But they also have to spend the right amount on data collection, analysis, and decision-making.

If they don't do a good job collecting data, filtering it, prioritizing it and combining it with existing knowledge, they won't make the right decision. If they don't make the right decision, it doesn't matter how much they spend on action. They're doing the wrong thing.

Moving through the Data-Analysis-Decision-Action chain smartly is the key.

If you're not going through this chain smartly in your daily life, it's not good. But when conflict comes and you don't think smartly, it's worse.

If you're still collecting or analyzing data while others are acting, you're in trouble.

There was no weapon in the druggie's hands.

It was a diversion. A distraction. A way to make sure I didn't see the real threat.

He had given me new data. When his hands moved, I looked for weapons. While I focused on his hands and what was in them, he was doing something else. It's a classic strategic move. What John Boyd called getting inside the other side's loop.

The druggie was moving his head. His forehead, specifically. In a downward motion. Snapped forward by his neck.

The forehead is a hard bone. Designed to protect the brain.

It's also a weapon.

His forehead landed on my left eyebrow.

My balance was thrown off. I fell.

Wet, sticky stuff on my face. My fingers came away red. Blood.

Head wounds bleed. All those vessels going to the brain. Carrying nutrients so you can think. Which I hadn't.

I was back where I started. Back in my seat with a druggie standing over me.

This time, with blood in an eye. This time, my options were more limited.

Only two.

4

How To Think About Others

I was bleeding. A little stunned. But I hadn't lost yet.

I still had the phone.

And two options:

1. Stay down

2. Get up again.

He had struck first. Knocked me down. Made me bleed. And it hurt.

But he hadn't knocked me out. Thankfully, I was looking down when it happened. With my chin tucked in, my neck was stronger. Stabilized my head. Kept it from twisting. Kept me conscious.

Looking down had been the wrong move. But it had

also saved me from something worse.

I was functioning. Not thinking, just functioning. Not thinking enough to gather more data and analyze it. But functioning enough. Enough to make a decision. The last decision I would make in the fight.

When he came at me again, I wouldn't be lying down. I started to get up.

Before I could, the druggie did something else I didn't expect. Something I wouldn't have guessed in a million years.

Let's take another look at the Iraq WMD situation. Before the war. In 2002. And let's look at the thinking of a person everyone considered crazy at the time: Saddam Hussein.

If you remember, the U.S. wanted Saddam Hussein to destroy his stockpiles of WMD. Hounded him for a decade. Got the UN involved. Sent inspectors. Generated resolution after resolution calling on Saddam Hussein to prove to the world he had no WMD.

As far as the U.S. was concerned, the ultimate game

was: Saddam Hussein gives up his WMD or he doesn't. If he doesn't, we go to war. One Zero-Sum Game (Saddam gets rid of WMD) or another (war). His choice.

Saddam Hussein chose war. Why?

To Saddam Hussein's thinking, the ultimate game wasn't with the U.S. In fact, it wasn't even with the U.N. Or the international community. In the ranking of enemies Saddam Hussein cared about, the U.S. and the U.N. weren't even in the top two.

Saddam Hussein's top enemies were internal. If you know Iraqi history, you know Saddam Hussein's party came to power in a coup. When he rose to the top, he had many of his own party members executed. He put down several attempts on his life over the years. He almost never slept two nights in the same place. Iraqi politics was the harshest kind of Zero-Sum Game. Losing the game equaled losing your life.

Saddam Hussein's second-most important game? Also Zero-Sum, but not internal. It was against Iran. In the 1980s, Iran and Iraq fought a brutal border war. Tens of thousands killed. Chemical weapons used. Any day, to Saddam Hussein's mind, war with Iran could happen again. What was Saddam Hussein's strategy for winning these two Zero-Sum Games? It was complicated. Confusing to outsiders. With many levels. But if you

---

understood the games he was playing and how he was thinking, what Saddam Hussein did with WMD made sense.

After the war, an FBI agent interrogated Saddam Hussein about WMD. The FBI agent summed up Saddam Hussein's answers this way: "Hussein believed that Iraq could not appear weak to its enemies, especially Iran." What?

The short answer: Saddam Hussein wanted Iran to think he had WMD in order to deter attacks. But he didn't want anyone inside Iraq to actually possess WMD. Because whoever had the WMD inside Iraq could use it to threaten Saddam Hussein's grip on power.

Saddam Hussein created a perception of having stockpiles of WMD without actually having much (he had some). That worked, as long as the games against his internal opposition and Iran were the most important games. When it came time to fight a third Zero-Sum Game against the U.S. and an international coalition, that strategy backfired.

Saddam Hussein had to choose between winning his top two games (against internal opposition and Iran) and fighting a battle against the U.S. (against whom he had lost before, but afterward, stayed in power).

As most people do, Saddam Hussein decided to handle the more immediate threats first. That led to three decisions that ultimately meant his life:

1. Don't allow international inspectors to see he had very little WMD.

2. Don't allow anyone internally to know he had very little WMD.

3. Fight the U.S.-led international coalition.

I was bleeding on the subway seat but still in the fight. One working eye on the druggie, I gathered myself. Got ready to stand up.

That's when it came.

A high-pitched howl. Like a wolf baying at the moon.

The druggie's face contorted into a smile.

It was so strange, so out of context, I didn't recognize it at first. Then I understood.

He was laughing.

The druggie laughed and laughed. Like the funniest

thing he'd ever seen was me bleeding on the seat.

Then he turned. Still facing me, still laughing, he walked backward down the subway car aisle. Sat down. Turned sideways and looked at me.

Still laughing.

I stood up, a hand pressed to my forehead. A couple more beats of my heart, and my fingers were dripping with blood. No way to stop it. Everything sticky. Everything red.

I checked my coat pocket for the phone. Still there. Glanced at the seat behind me to be sure I hadn't dropped anything.

I got off at the next stop. Half the car emptied out. Probably the last stop for only a few. The rest didn't want to be on a subway car with a laughing druggie lunatic who'd just made me bleed.

The young man in front of me got off, too. The one I thought might have been an ally. He came up and asked in the local language if I was all right.

I was glad to hear the local language. Because it answered the first question I always asked: Did he know I was a spy? The answer: No.

I was fine, I told him. But I must have looked bad,

because he offered to take me somewhere. I thanked him again, said no. I'd be fine.

I climbed to street level. Took a crosswalk, and the first people coming toward me are local cops. Blood all over me and trying to blend in, they're the last people I want to see. They'll ask questions. Want to see ID. I was functioning, not thinking. Not wanting a test of my cover story.

They took a close look at me. One of them started to stop. But the other nudged him forward. They walked past. Maybe it was the end of their shift. Maybe they didn't want to deal with the blood.

The rest of the morning had smaller hurdles. In my office, the alarm wouldn't reset. Had to wake up a colleague to come babysit my stuff. Sat for two hours with Band-Aids and a cold rag.

When I got to the hospital, I had a cover story to tell the doctor. Why I was cut. What happened. But I didn't have to use it – no one asked why I had a two inch gash on my forehead. They just stitched me up. No need for general anesthetic, which I would have refused. Just a couple of pricks, a bunch of stitches and it was over.

When I made it to the backup meeting with the source, he was fine. A little concerned I had missed the first meeting, but not too worried. He was a crusty guy. Been through the wars. Understood the random difficulties of being a spy. A little cut over the eye? No big deal, in the grand scheme.

And I hadn't lost the phone. In the Zero-Sum conflict, I hadn't won anything. But I hadn't lost anything, either. Status quo was the result. Fine by me.

My wife looked over the stitches when I got home. Made sure they were tight. "It's not too bad," she said. "Could've been worse."

Thinking is what this short book is about. We've talked about two tools that help. The Data-Analysis-Decision-Action chain helps us focus on where we might have holes in our thinking. Have we gathered the right data? Are we analyzing it correctly? Are we making the right decisions, as a result? Are our actions in line with our decisions?

The Positive-Sum/Zero-Sum/Negative-Sum framework helps us think ahead.

Now we'll use both to talk about the one thing you

and I both know: this book. Or more specifically, your decision to buy this short book (assuming you did) and my decision to write it.

I'll start. First, I had to look ahead. Was there a Positive-Sum Game out there to play? Was there an opportunity to create something that others would benefit from? That they'd pay for voluntarily?

My hypothesis was yes. If I wrote this, people like you would be interested. You'd even be willing to pay to read it.

To test that hypothesis, I had several questions. What kinds of spy books sell? How about books about thinking?

To answer, I gathered data. Not too difficult, with internet reviews, sales figures and the fact that writers love nothing more than writing about writing.

Analyzing that data, I noted the kinds of books people like to buy. The kinds of books that get good reviews. Books that aren't too long. Books with short sentences. Books that get a message across in an interesting way.

Final analysis: This kind of book has a chance, if I do it right. A chance to be bought. A chance to be read. Decision made: Write the book.

Acting on that decision was costly and time-consuming, including time for the CIA to approve it. Ultimately, it was completed. I wrote it and made it available for you to buy.

A graphic of the process:

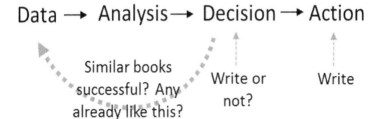

Data → Analysis → Decision → Action

Similar books successful? Any already like this?

Write or not?

Write

Now, your side. You, at some point, were presented with a decision on whether to buy this book (or steal it or borrow it) or not. You gathered data to make the decision. Maybe you read online reviews. Maybe you talked to someone who had read it. Maybe it wasn't really your decision: a teacher forced you to buy it.

You evaluated that data, judged its credibility and combined it with what you already know. You know that spy stories are generally interesting. You also know, if you've read any books by actual spies, that true spy stories can be dull. So you're reluctant. Or maybe you looked at the title and thought it was a little overdone.

"A guide to thinking and strategy? Really?"

You also looked at the price and the time needed to read it and wondered if the book was worth the cost. Eventually you decided it was. Decision made: Buy the book.

In our modern world, turning that decision into action isn't too hard. Just a click or two, usually.

So you did it. You bought the book. And you've read it this far.

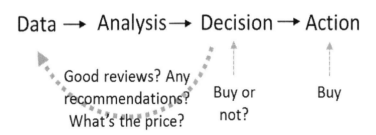

Data → Analysis → Decision → Action

Good reviews? Any recommendations? What's the price?

Buy or not?

Buy

Since you bought the book, and I wrote it, we both win. A Positive-Sum Game, assuming you liked it. You get the stories and the knowledge in this book. A greater value, hopefully, than what you paid for it. I get the money. A greater value in aggregate, hopefully, than what it cost me to write it.

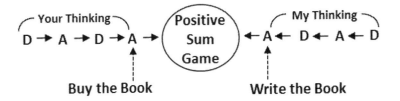

If both of us are acting in a Positive-Sum Game, we both win. I've written the book. You've paid for it. I get paid. You get tools that work. We both win.

Now, it's time to move on to our next game. Another Positive-Sum Game, hopefully.

The next game is about strategy.

5

Strategy

"What people do affects what other people do." – Thomas Schelling

He told me a lie.

And then, more lies. A whole bunch of lies.

But that wasn't the problem.

Lies are normal, when you're a spy.

The problem was that it was the wrong kind of lie.

Usually, a spy's lies:

1. Conceal something and/or;

---

2. Protect the spy.

Sometimes, a spy's lies do both. But these lies didn't. They didn't do either one. They did the opposite.

The lies exposed him. And didn't protect him. The lies made things more dangerous.

Not just dangerous for him. Dangerous for me, too.

Which made me wonder if it was an accidental lie. Maybe it was a heat-of-the-moment kind of lie. Maybe it was an emotional lie. Maybe he lied from embarrassment. Or shame. Or insecurity.

Then, after he lied once, he had to lie again. And the second and third and fourth lies were told for the usual reasons. To conceal the first lie. To protect him.

Maybe that's what happened.

Whatever the reason, I had to do something about it.

He had lied. Now, it was my turn to act.

It was my turn to do something about it.

But first, I wanted to understand why. I wanted to understand the decision behind the lies.

You see the action of a lie and you take a step back in the Data-Analysis-Decision-Action sequence. You look at the decision to lie.

Then a step further back. What were his choices?

Then a step further back. What analysis led to that decision?

Then another step back. What information or data did he analyze to make the decision that led to that action?

Then you go back to the action and take a step forward.

What result did he expect from lying?

You look at intent.

Like the courts do. They dole out different punishments depending on why something happened. When someone gets killed, the courts want to know why.

They want to know intent.

Accidental? Negligent? If so, third-degree. A crime of passion? If so, second-degree. Maybe third. Malice aforethought? Cold-blooded and pre-meditated? First-degree. The worst kind.

It doesn't matter if the initial crime was third-degree if a worse one followed. You get judged on the worst one. If there was first-degree crime to cover up a third-degree crime, you're judged on the first-degree crime.

Which he had done. Whichever way they started out, his lies had become first-degree.

They were done on purpose.

Which meant intent.

And his intent mattered for a practical reason.

His intent was a clue to what he would do next.

I wanted to know how he would approach our next meeting. Would he come as a friend? Or an enemy? Or with a bunch of his friends, who would be a bunch of my enemies?

What would he do next?

A strategic question.

A strategic question because what he would do next mattered for what I would do next.

With strategic questions, you game them out. You predict what the other side will do if you do X. If you do Y, you imagine how they'll respond. You put it all together and choose the best path forward.

You build a strategy.

Which isn't difficult, if there's a predictable path for

the other side.

Which there wasn't. Because there was a wrinkle with the lying source.

A wrinkle that took away the predictable path. A wrinkle that made it difficult to build a strategy.

The wrinkle was that the lying source knew that I knew he had lied.

He knew he had been caught. He knew that I knew.

Which meant he was thinking about what I would do next. He was thinking about whether I would do bad things.

He was thinking of worst-case scenarios.

He was thinking strategically, too.

Which meant he could deviate from a predictable path. And probably would.

Which was dangerous.

Because the worst-case scenarios in his head came from spy movies. From what spies in the movies would do. James Bond. Jason Bourne. Jack Bauer.

He had seen them all. He liked to quote them to me. He liked to compare what they did to what we were doing.

Which was a problem.

Movie spies hurt people. Sometimes, movie spies kill people. Sometimes, movie spies blow up whole villages. For less than what he'd done.

Now, he was gaming out what I would do. Would I hurt him? Worse: Kill him? Worse still: Hurt his family?

I wouldn't. But he didn't know that.

Which was a problem.

A strategic problem.

After all, this guy wasn't a bureaucrat. He wasn't a businessman. He wasn't a normal guy.

He was a tough guy. Professionally.

He'd been in fights. Fights he'd won. Fights he'd lost.

He knew what fighters know: Whoever strikes first usually wins.

If he thought a fight was coming, he'd make the first move.

He'd strike first.

Which meant I had two choices:

1. Wait for him to strike, or;

2. Strike before he did.

Which he knew.

If he thought I'd choose option 2, he'd go sooner. He'd strike before I could.

Which I knew.

It would be the logic of first strikes.

If we both thought a fight was coming, a fight was a certainty.[2] One of us would strike as soon as there was a chance.

Dangerous.

Which I knew. And he did, too.

Which meant I needed a good strategy.

For that, I had to see his strategy.

Because I missed it the first time.

I missed it completely.

For most of the 20th century, it was good to be an American. It was better being an American than being an African. Or an Asian. It was better than being from South America. Much better than being from Europe.

Then came the early 2000s, and it was especially good.

The Cold War was over. The Berlin Wall was gone. No risk of nuclear strikes. No concerns about invasion. No existential threats.

Plus, American influence was spreading. Which brought trade and technology and access to new horizons. Which meant it was even better to be an American. Conflicts were fading. Wealth was exploding, if you were an American.

There was still greed and ambition and market crashes and rogue states, but the trend was positive. For Americans, things were getting better.

Until 9/11.

The Twin Towers fell. The Pentagon was struck. Heroes died in a Pennsylvania field.

For the first time in a long time, outsiders had killed Americans on American soil.

Everybody knew somebody who was killed.

For me, it was a guy who lived next door in college. His girlfriend dropped him at the Twin Towers twenty minutes before the first plane hit.

After they hit, she tried to call him. She got nothing. She stayed in Midtown hoping for a return call. She watched the buildings collapse and hoped he stopped for coffee. She watched the dust rise and prayed something had kept him in the lobby so he could escape. She hoped he had done anything except take the express elevator to the 101st floor.

But he took the elevator. We know he got to his desk. We know he was on the 101st floor when the planes hit.

After that, we don't know what happened. Maybe he died from the smoke. Maybe he was crushed in the stairwell. Maybe he jumped.

No one knows what happened, except that he was gone.

With so many others.

The grief came in stages. Denial. Anger. Bargaining. Depression. Acceptance.

But not everyone got through the stages. Some got stuck on anger.

No bargaining. No depression. No acceptance.

Just anger.

Anger was fuel for the war to come.

But not the normal kind of war.

A "war on terror," it was called.

But terror isn't an enemy. Terror isn't even a strategy.

Terror is a tactic.

Terror is a tool of war. It's a small part of a larger game.

Which confused a lot of people. Many Americans didn't know we were at war. Many Americans didn't know why 9/11 happened. Why terror was used. Why we had an enemy.

But none of that mattered at first.

All that mattered was that enemies existed. All that mattered was that enemies had attacked us. Enemies had killed our people.

It was time to fight back.

The CIA was ready.

The CIA was ready because we had fought the enemy already. In the Middle East. In Africa. We had been bloodied in bombings.

But 9/11 was different. It happened on American soil and innocents had died. Thousands of innocents. It was time to fight back.

The CIA's Cofer Black, Gary Schroen, and Gary Berntsen took a plan off the shelf. And bags of cash. Rounded up every intelligence source they could. Partnered with Afghan Forces. Worked with the Special Forces to track down our enemies.

A guy in the training class ahead of me went with them. A former Marine, he was in the Special Activities Division.[3] He was trained up. Ready to go.

He went to Afghanistan. In a prison, he was acquiring intelligence. There was an uprising. The prisoners attacked him. He died when he had no more bullets. His name was Mike Spann.

Thousands dead in New York, Washington and Pennsylvania. And one of our own in Afghanistan.

The hard work continued.

The enemy leader Bin Laden was found. Cornered at Tora Bora. Then, he escaped.

Into the tribal areas. A desolate landscape. From the sky, it looked like another planet.

With Bin Laden's escape, the war took a turn. A new

---

phase.

A phase where the enemy was still a threat, but contact was limited.

Like boxing in the dark. We tried to get close. But the enemy backed away. We threw punches, but few landed. He shifted and stayed out of reach.

Which meant it was time to rethink our strategy.

Rethinking our strategy meant understanding Bin Laden's strategy.

Which few understood in the early days.

Few understood why Bin Laden had attacked on 9/11. Few understood why Bin Laden started a war with the United States.

Few understood why Bin Laden sent 19 men on a suicide mission into the United States. Few understood why Bin Laden had killed so many. Few could get inside Bin Laden's head.

Which meant few understood what Bin Laden would do next.

Few understood Bin Laden's strategy.

Which was important to understand.

Because Bin Laden was a formidable strategist.

When Bin Laden attacked the United States on 9/11, not only did he kill more Americans than any foreigner had for many, many years.

The attacks on 9/11 were strategically important.

The attacks on 9/11 advanced Bin Laden's strategy in eight significant ways.

When you're a spy, you see a lot of strategies.

You see the grand strategies. The worldwide strategies. The strategies of transnational movements. The strategies of global influence networks. Across space and time.

Then you zoom in. To one continent. To one time. Where nations collide. Where resources matter. Where histories matter. Where plans for revenge and restitution and glory become strategies.

Then you zoom in again. Within a nation. To factions. Political parties. Ethnic groups. And families. You see politics. You see groups teaming up with other groups

---

to pursue revolution and reward and independence.

Then you zoom in on an individual. A person.
Someone with dreams. And fears. And anger. And love.
Someone building a strategy to satisfy them all.

When you're a spy, you see a lot of strategies because
that's your job.

It's your job to see grand strategies. Regional
strategies. National strategies. Most of all, individual
strategies.

It's your job to see them and to understand them,
because that's how you know when threats exist.

To identify threats, you're infiltrating an enemy's
organization. You're figuring out who is making
decisions. And who isn't. You're collecting intelligence
on what they know. And what they don't know.

You're figuring out their plans. Whether they mean
you harm or don't. Whether they're a threat. Whether
they're going to attack. Hopefully, before it's done.

You're uncovering the enemy's strategy.

That's the job of a spy.

But it's not only enemies' strategies you see.

You're also talking to allies. Who have strategies of

---

their own. You're understanding what they want. What they don't. Hopefully, they'll tell you what their strategy is. But sometimes, they don't.

Then, there's your side's strategy.

Your side's strategy is why you're a spy. It's why they send you to foreign countries and back alleys and diplomatic receptions. You're there to serve your side's strategy.

When you're a spy, you have a front row seat to a lot of strategies.

Which means you see some strategies succeed.

And you see many more strategies fail.

Sometimes, a strategy fails because of logistics. Or because the enemy strikes first. Or because the strategy was overtaken by events. Or because it was made obsolete by inaction.

But most strategies fail earlier. Most strategies fail before a conflict starts. Most strategies fail before an alliance is formed. Before even war is declared.

Most strategies fail because they're made the wrong way.

Most strategies fail because they don't follow what

game theorists Dixit and Nalebuff call the First Rule of Strategy.[4]

It's a simple rule: Look forward and reason backward.

Simple but difficult to do.

Unless you know a shortcut.

On 11 September at 9:25 a.m., American authorities shut down American airspace. By the time it and the airports reopened on 13 September, a second decision had been made: Boost security.

Which meant more security screeners in airports. More x-ray machines and explosives detection machines. More time examining passengers.

And then things calmed down. We mourned the dead. We tried to get back to life.

A month after 9/11, I was getting back to life. My wife and I took a trip to the American Midwest. We saw friends. we saw family. We reminded ourselves what was important. Why what we were doing was important.

Then it was time to get back to DC.

Traffic was bad on the way to the airport. Enough to make us late. The security line was long, so my wife left her bags with me. She got in the shorter line, breezed through security and ran to hold the plane.

I nudged the bags forward. Checked my watch. Inched to the conveyer. Finally loaded the luggage. Waited for the instruction. Stepped through the metal detector.

A security guard raised his palm. Told me to stop. Told me to remove my shoes.

He was young. No older than 20. Probably just a few weeks on the job.

No problem, I said.

I gave him my shoes.

He pointed to a chair. Told me to sit.

Everything in the security area was new. New people. New procedures. New machines.

No architectural changes yet. No roped off lanes. Everything and everybody crammed together. Old space for new things. Which meant everything was tight.

The chair I sat in was crammed behind a new explosives testing machine. The chair was probably used for workers' breaks most of the time. Its location was an afterthought. Also a mistake.

I had a full view of the testing machine's screen. The kind of machine where the round swipe cloth goes in a round receiver. On the screen were boxes with letters and numbers.

C4. TNT. PETN. And more. Maybe twenty types of explosives. Dull and waiting.

The security guard stood next to it and rubbed the swipe cloth over my shoes.

That's when it hit me.

I had worn those shoes before.

Four months before.

In explosives training. Before 9/11. Before airports started testing for explosives on shoes.

My heart pumped. My vision tunneled. Adrenaline flowed, slowing time.

It was time to think. Which wasn't easy.

It wasn't easy because I didn't want to think. I wanted to move.

Adrenaline had primed the pump. My breathing had

quickened. My muscles had tightened. My body wanted to move.

Which would have been bad.

Moving would bring all of airport security down on me.

So I sat.

And took a deep breath.

And tried to think.

The round cloth went over the shoe laces. Down along the side. Across the rubber sole. And back to the top. In slow motion.

In slow motion, the round cloth picked up lots of microscopic residue of explosive material.

A conflict was coming. A conflict with ripple effects.

Getting caught with explosives residue by an airport screener in the Midwest would not be good.

Not good for getting back to DC quickly. Not good for my wife holding the plane. Not good for my career at the CIA.

I needed a strategy.

I looked forward.

———————————————

I looked to the conflict coming with security. But also past it. To the effects of failure. Which I wanted to avoid.

So I looked past failure. To the outcome I wanted.

And then I reasoned backward.

From the outcome I wanted back to now.

In seconds, the security area would shut down.

All attention would be on me.

Ten seconds.

The young security screener put the round cloth in the testing machine.

I looked forward again to the outcome I wanted.

Five seconds.

I reasoned backward from the outcome I wanted back to now.

One second.

I built a strategy.

Then the explosives testing machine lit up.

The lying source had volunteered.

Which I appreciated. You can save time with volunteers. You can vet more quickly. You can get intelligence more quickly. You can move fast.

But you don't move too fast. Volunteers are the easiest way to expose you. A rival intelligence service can find out who you are. Worse, hit you with a double-agent.

In his background check, there were no red flags. But that didn't mean he wasn't a double-agent. It just meant that if he was a double-agent, he was a good one.

For the first meeting, I did all the normal things. Set the meeting location for a public place. Changed it.

I was already inside the restaurant when he entered.

He sat at a table, like he had been told. I let him sit. So I could analyze the data stream he produced.

He wore cheap nice clothes. Like he wasn't trying to impress. Or couldn't afford to. His shoes were worn. Dirty from walking. He sat in the chair like he wanted to be standing up. Like he wanted to move.

He was quick with his eyes. But not scared. Aware, not paranoid. Expectant and a little nervous. But not too nervous. Not sweating.

Not sweating like he had a layer of explosives wrapped around his chest. Which was good.

His shirt was loose. As he sat, there were no adjustments for hard things under his arm or on his ankle or in his belt.

No gun. No bombs. Good.

A dozen people cycled in and out. I let him sit long enough to test his patience. Long enough for him to glance at his watch. Long enough for something to happen, if something was going to happen.

Nothing happened.

I walked up to him sideways. Kept an eye on his hands. Generously, he kept them on the table.

I said his name, and he focused on me. Which was good. No glancing around. No concern for others. All the attention on me.

I sat down. Made eye contact and smiled. Then, I ignored him. I looked around to see how others reacted to what I had done.

Some had watched me. Their eyes on me briefly. Which was normal. It was unusual for someone to move from one table to another. So they wondered why, naturally. But no one wondered too long. No one was there for me. No one was there for him.

But that was just a hypothesis. So I tested it. I picked out the guy who had watched the longest. He had entered after the volunteer. He had a nice view of our table. If anyone was here for us, it was him.

I stared at him. Long enough to make him uncomfortable. He looked at me. Didn't try to ignore me.

I watched the wheels turn in his head. He tried to place me. Tried to figure out why I was staring. Then he gave up. He looked away.

All clear. Back to the volunteer.

The first conversation with a potential source you make as relaxed as possible. Like a business introduction. Or a job interview. A get-to-know-you.

We talked about who he was. Where he was from. Who his family was. What he did for a living. Then, to business.

Why did you contact us? I asked.

"I want to help. I watched the Twin Towers fall. It was terrible. All the death. All the . . . destruction. A terrible day. I want to help. I want to help. To make certain it doesn't happen again."

Nice, but not great. 9/11 was years before.

Why did you wait? Why now? I asked.

"I wasn't able to help. I had wanted to, but I had other things . . . I wasn't able to. But now I can help, if you think I can help."

I asked about his job. The things he had been doing.

He launched into stories. Which was good.

Stories contain data. Filtered by choices. You learn what the storyteller values. What they think about others. Most importantly, what they think about themselves. Are they the hero? A distant observer? A victim?

"I was working security," he said. "Protecting an important person. A meeting went bad. Guns came out. I got our guy in the backseat. My body on him. The driver hit the gas. We got away."

Did you fire your weapon? I asked.

"No," he said, a little disappointed.

Anyone hurt? I asked.

"No," he grinned. "When we stopped a few miles away, I saw a taillight had been shot out. But that was all."

His grin stayed. Like he was feeling the adrenaline and relief all over again. Which he liked.

Which was a problem. It put him in a category. A category that could be trouble. Not the hero category. Not the distant observer category. Not the victim category.

The tough guy category.

Tough guys cut a wide path. They leave behind taillight glass and shell casings and bodies. Everyone knows they were there.

When you're a spy, you don't want that. You want no one to know you were there. You avoid shootouts. You bypass bloodshed. You're in and out without anyone knowing.

But the tough guy category was just a hypothesis. Maybe he wasn't really a tough guy. Maybe he was a wannabe tough guy. Worse, maybe he wanted me to think he was a tough guy.

Either way, not promising. If he was lying about being a tough guy, it was a problem. If he was telling the truth about being a tough guy? That was a problem, too.

It could have been enough for me to say, Thank you very much. It could have been enough to walk away.

I didn't.

I didn't because it was just one meeting. I had hypotheses, but I hadn't tested them.

I moved on to secrecy.

Who did you tell about contacting us?

"Nobody," he said.

Nobody? I repeated.

A little nervousness on his face, but not much. "Nobody," he said.

Good, I said.

I asked more questions. He answered with more stories.

Which gave me more hypotheses about him. Hypotheses I could test.

Hypothesis #1: He's a straight-up volunteer. He's not a double-agent.

Hypothesis #2: He has enough access to information to be helpful.

I tested Hypothesis #1 first.

Strategy starts when you look forward.

Which requires imagination.

It looks like this:

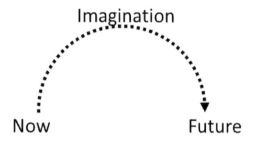

Imagination is easy for most people. It's easy to imagine a future. To imagine a place. To imagine people in it. The things in it.

Which means people do the first part of strategy all the time.

It's the next part that's more difficult.

The next part of strategy is reasoning backward.

It looks like this:

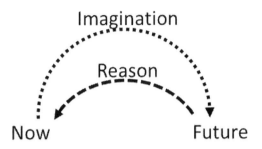

Reasoning backward is more difficult because we usually do things forward.

We imagine forward. We act forward. We live forward. We think from here to there. From now to the future.

Which makes sense. Most people wouldn't think of doing anything backward.

But reasoning backward is important. It's the key to a good strategy. It's how you build strategies. It's how you plan when you're a spy.

When you're a spy, source meetings are everything. Meetings are where you develop and recruit. Meetings are where you get intelligence. Meetings are where you're at risk. Meetings are where you connect with the source.

The most important part of a meeting is that it happens. If a meeting doesn't happen, you don't develop and recruit. If it doesn't happen, you don't get intelligence.

To make sure meetings happen, you spend a lot of time planning. You plan so there's time to detect surveillance. You plan so there's extra time for unexpected events. You plan so you get to the meeting safely on time.

When you're planning, you don't start where you are today. You don't start at now.

You plan backwards.

You start at the meeting time and location. As you plan, you treat the meeting time and location like it's fixed. Like it can't be changed. Like it's everything.

You start in the future. And reason backward.

If the meeting is in a Sao Paolo café on a Wednesday in June, you reason backward from there.

You look at which hotels are the right distance from the café to allow a good surveillance detection run. You pick one.

Then you go backward again. You look at which airports are best to get you to the hotel. You pick one.

You go backward again. You pick a flight that gets you to the airport. And backward through transportation and stops along the way. All the way back to where you are now. Weeks or months before the meeting.

You reasoned backward.

You built a strategy.

And then you do it.

You act.

Put imagination, reason and action together, and it looks like this:

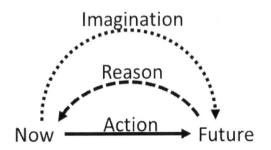

You imagined your future.

You reasoned backward.

Then you acted.

Of the three steps, imagination and action are usually easiest. Imagination and action are what most people do every day. Imagination and action go forward. The way most people are used to going.

But reasoning goes backward.

Which is why most people don't do it.

Plus, reasoning backward is complex. It's complicated. It's unwieldy. It takes more effort. It takes more time. It takes practice to get it right.

But reasoning backward is essential.

Reasoning backward ties together imagination and action.

Without reasoning backward, you're shooting in the dark. You're imagining and acting along a path that may not makes sense. You're putting yourself at risk.

Without reasoning backward, you'll end up with a bad strategy.

Which is dangerous, when you're a spy. When you're a spy, a bad strategy is risky. A bad strategy means you took risk for nothing. A bad strategy can mean you get arrested. Or worse.

When you're a spy, you take the time to reason backward. You make the effort to reason backward. You practice reasoning backward.

So you can do it quickly and efficiently.

Even when you only have a few seconds.

In the summer of 2001, I watched things explode.

Cars blew apart. Old tanks exploded. Busted metal flew through the air.

At detonation, we were behind thick glass. Inside a half-buried concrete bunker. Just in case busted metal flew toward us.

After the explosion, we waited. Someone had already done the math. Someone knew how long it was until all the busted metal in the air landed. A timer counted down. At zero, we went to see what happened.

In the open air were clouds of fine dust. Tiny grains of explosives in the air. Tiny grains of explosive chemicals landed in my hair. Covered my clothes. Coated my skin.

And stuck to my shoes.

If you're near an explosion, your shoes get residue all over them. Not just from the air. Also from the dirt. You walk near an explosion, and your shoes are covered in microscopic explosive residue.

Which is what happened to the shoes I wore to the airport weeks after 9/11. The shoes were covered in microscopic explosive residue. The shoes the security guard was testing.

In the weeks after 9/11, my assignment had changed. I moved from an assignment with a long-term payoff to one focused on the immediate need of counterterrorism. A big adjustment. Different training. Different work.

But I hadn't fully adjusted. I hadn't thought through all the new risks. I hadn't thought about the shoes I was wearing.

A stupid mistake.

A rookie mistake.

Now an airport security officer was testing my shoes. Shoes with explosives residue all over them.

It was trouble. Not life and death trouble. No one would die because I had microscopic explosive residue on my shoes. But it wasn't good.

If I didn't resolve this quickly, my bosses would hear about it. Which they would love. Spy bosses love unexpected tests for new spies. Because they get to see how you react under pressure.

Getting caught by a Midwestern airport security guard with explosives on my shoes was a great test. A natural test. If I failed, there would be consequences. Consequences I wanted to avoid.

Which meant it was time to build a strategy.

Not a grand strategy. Not a world-encompassing strategy. A small strategy. An individual strategy. A micro-strategy that got me through the situation without embarrassment.

I started at the end.

At the end, I would get on the plane with my wife. Go back to DC. My bosses never find out I got caught with explosives residue on my shoes.[5]

That's what I imagined. That's what I wanted.

Then to reason backward. To the step just before I went to the plane. When someone with authority in the security area released me. Someone higher than the security guard testing my shoes.

That person would need to have a reason to release me. I reasoned backward from there. A couple more steps. Back to where I was.

Back to now.

Back to sitting behind the explosives detection machine. Watching the security guard inserting the testing circle. Waiting for the alarm to go off.

I built a strategy. Backward.

The action would be: I would tell a story. A story that gave me a good chance of going free. If my bosses were called in, the story wouldn't upset airport security. In fact, it would impress them.

The story was plausible. Close to the truth. But not exactly the truth. And not exactly a lie. Most importantly, no need to mention the CIA.

I ran through the story to test for holes.

No holes. I was ready.

That's when the screen on the explosives testing machine lit up.

Every single bar lit up.

Every single kind of explosive. TNT. C4. PETN. And many more. Now lit, I could see there were some explosives on my shoes I had never heard of. Even in training.

"Holy S---," said the security guard.

He sprinted to his supervisor. Pointed at me. The supervisor made a signal. A siren went off. In two seconds, the security area was shut down.

The supervisor gathered his people. In a huddle. Like a football team getting the play. Occasionally a head popped up. Looked at me.

I tried to look sheepish. Innocent as a dove.

Meanwhile, I ran through the story again. I anticipated questions. Looked for holes.

It was pretty good, I thought: I was working in Washington. I'd done a public tour of the FBI's facility at Quantico. Part of the tour had been where the FBI does explosives training. I walked through that area with these shoes.

It would make sense to the airport security supervisor. Even gain his respect. Because everybody wants to move up in the world. For an airport security supervisor, the FBI would be higher in the hierarchy.

_____

That I had been to Quantico? Instant respect. And no need to mention the CIA.

Plus, it was partly true. I had been to Quantico. But the visit hadn't been public. And I hadn't worn these shoes. But that didn't matter.

The huddle broke up. The supervisor came over. A phalanx of security personnel behind him. Like an American football team approaching the line of scrimmage. A little jog in his step. Everyone fanned out behind him.

He was an older guy. Gray at the tips. The kind of guy who takes his job seriously. He takes his community seriously. Probably volunteers as a Little League coach. The kind of guy who doesn't yell at his players. He sits them down instead.

That's how it felt when he spoke to me. It felt like a sit-down.

"I'm sorry, son," he said. "We're going to have to run your shoes through the x-ray again."

Or maybe I was wrong. Maybe he was a clever guy. Maybe he was a retired detective. Maybe he adopted the coach persona because it gets people to confess. And maybe now he was going to let me stew. See if I got nervous.

I said, Of course, sir. No problem.

My wife would be waiting at the gate. Thinking I was just behind her. Arguing with somebody to hold the flight. Hopefully winning.

The supervisor ran my shoes through the x-ray machine. The shoes came out clean, as they should. As they would if they actually had explosives in them. Easy to make certain explosives look like a shoe sole on an x-ray.

The supervisor told me to stand up. Waved me toward the x-ray machine. If he was a retired detective, I was ready for my interrogation.

I had the story ready. Two levels of questions deep. When had I gone to Quantico? Who was my contact there? Who had organized the visit? Why had I been invited? What was my job? I hoped it wouldn't go three questions deep.

Instead, the supervisor handed me a clipboard.

He said, "Son, I'm going to need you to write your flight number here."

I stared at him. A trick? No questions about who I was? Nothing about the explosives residue?

I dug out my ticket. Found the flight number. Wrote it

down. Handed it to the supervisor. Waited.

He looked at the clipboard.

Looked at me.

"You can take your shoes now," he said. "Have a nice flight."

Maybe the supervisor wasn't a coach or a retired detective. Maybe he was just trying to get as many people through the security area as quickly as possible. And despite the explosives machine being right, he didn't think I was a threat.

Whatever he thought, I was free. My wife won the argument with the gate agent. I boarded the plane. They shut the doors behind me. I dropped into my seat.

I switched into a second pair of shoes. When we arrived in DC, the shoes with explosives residue went in the first trash can I saw.

That was it.

No one contacted me after. No one asked me why I had explosives residue all over my shoes.

That was it.

If a guy with explosives residue all over his shoes was let through airport security, there was a problem with American counterterrorism tactics in the months after 9/11.[6]

Which means there was a problem with American counterterrorism strategy.

Tactics are action. Tactics are what you do to make a strategy real. Without tactics, strategy doesn't matter.

After 9/11, the U.S. beefed up airport security. Poured resources in. Sometimes it was effective. As I found it, sometimes it wasn't.

But it wasn't just airports that needed protection.

The United States is a big place. With lots of soft targets. Lots of shopping malls. Lots of stadiums. Lots of parks. Lots of vulnerable places.

Which was a problem after 9/11. A strategic problem. With so many soft targets, you can't watch over them all. You can't protect them all.

In the months after 9/11, many Americans stayed away from shopping malls. Away from stadiums. Away from public spaces.

They waited for Bin Laden to strike again.

They waited for attacks to come.

But the attacks never came.

Why?

Attacks come when an enemy has two things:

1. The capability to attack.

2. The will to attack.

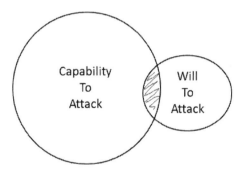

After 9/11, the U.S. strategy was to reduce Bin Laden's capability to attack.

Billions of dollars and millions of hours and hundreds of lives went into one thing: Making sure Bin Laden never had the *capability* to attack the U.S. again.

But there was also the second thing: the will to attack again.

Did Bin Laden have the *will* to attack the United States again?

A ridiculous question, some would say. Maybe, an offensive question.

Of course, Bin Laden wanted to attack us again.

After all, Bin Laden had attacked us once. Clearly, he had the *will* to attack.

But if you're building a strategy, you don't assume the enemy will do what they did last time. You don't assume that because they did something once they'll do it again. You don't assume the enemy will do the obvious.

You assume the enemy will do what advances their strategy. You assume the enemy will do what they have the capability and the will to do.

You assume the enemy has looked forward.

You assume the enemy has reasoned backward.

You assume the enemy has a strategy.

You assume the enemy will act in line with their strategy.

They'll attack when they have the capability and the will to attack. When it fits their strategy.

To predict and prevent attacks, you need to understand the other side's strategy.

So when they act, you're ready.

So when they act, you know what to do.

So when they act, you've got a strategy of your own.

6

Games

"It may not be enough to play a game well—you must also be sure you are playing the right game." – Avinash Dixit

When you're a spy, you hide in plain sight.

You act like a consultant. Or a bureaucrat. Or a technician. You act like something you're not. In plain sight.

You have the right glasses. You have the right haircut. You have the right underwear, in case you get searched.

You look right. You act right. To anyone wondering who you are, everything feels right.

At a border crossing, you answer questions. As boringly as possible. So they move on. So they think there's no reason to stop you. Because you're hiding in plain sight.

But no matter how good you are at hiding in plain sight, there are two moments that can trip you up.

Moment #1: When you go from your real life to another identity.

Moment #2: When you go back.

In those moments, the best acting job won't save you. In those moments the right haircut, glasses and underwear won't save you. In those moments, your answers are worthless.

If a security service sees you in those moments, it's over.

There's only possibility: You're a spy.

Which is why security services watch for those two moments.

If they see you living your real life, they'll watch for you to take on a different identity. If they suspect your identity isn't real, they'll watch for the moment when you go back to your real life.

Which is why spies watch for surveillance. Always. Everywhere. Obsessively.

You're always watching for people watching you.

Whether you're in a business meeting. Or on vacation. Or picking up the dog from the vet.

You use reflective surfaces. You funnel possible surveillants through chokepoints. You use vehicles and subways and walking paths. You use crowds where you blend in and empty spaces where surveillants are exposed. You make it so no one can follow you without you knowing.

And then you meet a source. A third risky moment.

A third risky moment because if the source was under surveillance, now you are, too.

I started the second meeting with the source there. As a partial test of Hypothesis #1. The one about him being a straight-up volunteer. Not a double-agent.

Were you followed? I asked.

"No," he said. "No, I wasn't."

How do you know? I asked.

"Because I know I wasn't," he said. Frustrated. Like it was a waste of time. Like he didn't need to worry about being followed.

A bad sign.

Which meant one of two things:

1. He was a double-agent, after all. Double-agents don't need to worry about being followed.

2. He was careless.

If he was a double-agent, he would at least act like he was worried. Because that's what a double-agent would do. At least, a good one would.

I chose the second option for my hypothesis: Careless.

Careless because there are more careless people in the world than double-agents. Even in the spy world.

But it was still just a hypothesis. To be tested again.

To be tested by the next thing we did.

But first, I wanted him to tell me more stories. More stories about his past. And maybe about what he wanted in the future. So I could understand what really motivated him to work with us.

I introduced some topics. Asked about his day job. Probed for his interests. All but begged him to tell me stories.

He gave one word answers. Each time, he turned the questions back on me. Back on what I would do. Back

———————————————

on what we were going to do. Back on next steps for our partnership.

He probed. In an obsessive, compulsive way. Like what we would do next was the most important thing in his life. Like he was desperate to do it. Like being a spy was everything.

Another bad sign.

Reasoning backward is difficult.

It's especially difficult when you're looking at grand strategies. World-encompassing strategies. Strategies that put all the players on one field. Strategies you see when you're a spy.

Fortunately, there's a shortcut.

A simple shortcut that helps you reason backward quickly. Efficiently. Accurately.

A shortcut that helps you understand others' strategies. And build your own.

The shortcut starts with a simple distinction:

Most strategic interactions are one of two kinds of "games."

In the first type of game, both sides win. Both sides are better off at the end than at the beginning. Or, at least, both sides go into the game expecting to benefit at the end.

The first type of game is a win-win game.

To make it work, both sides usually give something to the other side. Or trade something. Or exchange something. Or pool their resources. So something bigger is built. So they can share in something greater. So both sides win. It's a Positive-Sum Game.[7]

The second type of game is different. It's when only one side can win. At the end, only one side is better off. Which means one side isn't better off. The other side is worse off. The other side lost.

The second type of game is a win-lose game.

Totaling up the additions and subtractions at the end, you get zero. What is added to one side is taken from the other side. A plus for one is a minus for the other. It's a Zero-Sum Game.

Zero-Sum Games are competition or conflict over something. Maybe it's land. Or money. Or influence. Or a customer relationship. If one side wins it, the other side loses it.

There's a third kind of game, but it's rare. It's rare because both sides lose. Both sides are worse off at the end than they were at the beginning. It's a Negative-Sum Game.

If it's planned, a Negative-Sum Game is expected to be short. Like in a war of attrition. Because people can only stand to lose for so long. People want to return to Positive-Sum Games and Zero-Sum Games as quickly as they can.

The first two types of games happen all the time. In business. In war. In politics. In espionage. Even in friendships. Zero-Sum Games and Positive-Sum Games are everywhere.[8]

Which is helpful, because you can use them as a shortcut to reasoning backward.

It starts with this: Every Zero-Sum Game is fought over at least one of three things:

1. People, and/or;

2. Places, and/or;

3. Things

People, places, and/or things.[9]

What people fight over comes down to those three things. What people have wars and competitions and conflicts over comes down to those three things. Zero-Sum Games are always about people, places and/or things. What the winner gets is always people, places and/or things.

A Zero-Sum Game looks like this:

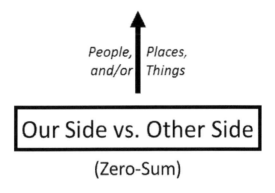

Whoever wins the Zero-Sum Game gets the people, places or things. Whoever loses the game loses the people, places or things.

Simple.

Positive-Sum Games are different. Different because they can't exist without people, places and things. Positive-Sum Games need what is fought over in Zero-Sum Games to exist.

Positive-Sum Games need three things:

1. People, and

2. A place, and

3. Things

Positive-Sum Games need all three.

A Positive-Sum Game looks like this:

(Positive-Sum)

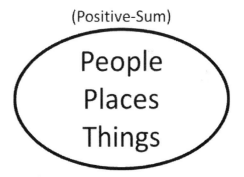

In strategy, you want to know which type of game you're playing.

Positive-Sum Game or Zero-Sum Game?

Is my interaction with this person competitive? Or friendly?

Will only one of us win? Or will we both be better off at the end?

It's difficult to know, sometimes. Especially, when you're a spy.

When you're a spy, it's an important question. Is this person across the table an enemy or ally? Betrayer or friend? Double agent or triple agent or worse?

Which type of game are we playing?

Fortunately, there's a way to answer.

A way to answer with the tools of strategy.

It starts the same way all strategy starts: You look forward and you reason backward.

But not for your side. You look forward and reason backward for the other side.

You look forward as if you were the other side. As if you were in their situation. In their place. With their people. Surrounded by their things. And you look forward.

You look forward as far as the other side can look.

You look forward until you reach the other side's Endgame.

And you reason backward from there.

Reasoning backward through the other side's strategy tells you if they'll be an ally or enemy. If they'll be a betrayer or friend. Or a double agent or triple agent or worse.

To understand the person across the table, you need to understand the types of games they want to play.

The type of game Bin Laden wanted to play with the U.S. was obvious: Zero-Sum.

He said it in fatwas. He said in videos and audio tapes. He even formally declared war. He called it "Declaration of War Against the Americans Occupying the Land of the Two Holy Places."

Which was strange.

Bin Laden said he was fighting for places.

Not people. Not things.

Places.

Holy Places for Bin Laden: Mecca and Jerusalem.

Americans had been in both for decades. Welcomed by locals in both for decades. But Bin Laden didn't like it. He said there was "no more important duty than pushing the American enemy out" of those Holy Places.

That's why he declared war against the United States.

At least, that's what he said.

To start the war, Bin Laden attacked U.S. interests overseas. In 1998, Bin Laden's followers bombed two American embassies in Africa. In 2000, they attacked the U.S.S. Cole in Yemen.

Then 9/11.

It was war.

On one side: Bin Laden. On the other side: The United States.

The U.S. vs. Bin Laden.

But a strange kind of war. Because if Bin Laden won, he wouldn't have what he said he was fighting for. Bin

Laden wouldn't have the Holy Places.

If Bin Laden won, the Saudis would still have Mecca. The Israelis would still have Jerusalem. Victory for Bin Laden wouldn't get Bin Laden what he said he wanted.

Which meant Bin Laden was a bad strategist or he didn't really want what he said he wanted.

Bin Laden wasn't a bad strategist.

Which made it a strange kind of war.

Nevertheless, it was a war.

It was a Zero-Sum Game. One side could win only what the other side lost.

It looked like this:

Bin Laden vs. U.S.

(Zero-Sum)

But it wasn't just the United States vs. Bin Laden.

It wasn't only a Zero-Sum Game.

Because both sides had an alliance.

And an alliance is a Positive-Sum Game.

It's rare that a single individual or country wins a war. Even hegemons need help. Which means everyone builds alliances before going to war.

Everyone plays the Positive-Sum Game of alliance to win the Zero-Sum Game of war.

If you were a German strategist in the late 19th century, you knew this. You knew Positive-Sum alliances win Zero-Sum wars.

You saw that a European war was coming. Conflict was inevitable. Soon would be a Zero-Sum Game over European people, places and things. One side would win. The other would lose.

You wanted to win, so you reasoned backward.

You knew you couldn't win the war on your own. Germany needed allies.

In Europe, there were five major powers: France, Russia, Austria-Hungary, Great Britain and Germany.[10]

Five major powers meant you wanted three on your

side. Because that meant the other side would have two. Three against two meant your alliance was bigger than the other side's alliance. When it came time for conflict, you'd probably win.

Otto von Bismarck knew this. He was Kaiser Wilhelm I's strategist. Bismarck did a lot of complicated diplomatic maneuvering from 1870-90 to make sure Germany always had two major powers as allies: Russia and Austria-Hungary. Together, the three powers were the Three Emperors' League.

Under Bismarck, the alliances of the five major European powers looked like this:

Bismarck's Europe

Three Emperors League vs. France + Great Britain

(Zero-Sum)

Three Emperors League

Germany
Austria-Hungary
Russia

(Positive-Sum)

France/Great Britain

France
Great Britain

(Positive-Sum)

Even better for Bismarck, the France-Great Britain alliance was weak. France and Great Britain didn't like each other. They weren't even friends.

When war came, Germany was in a strong position to win.

Then everything changed.

Kaiser Wilhelm I died. His grandson Wilhelm II eventually replaced him.

Wilhelm II didn't like alliances as much. In fact, they got in the way of what he really wanted: A Germany great on its own.

Bismarck saw the danger of going alone. Bismarck saw Germany wasn't strong enough to win against all the other European powers. Or even three.

If Germany had just one ally, Germany would probably lose. A European war would be three against two, with Germany one of the two.

Bismarck argued with Wilhelm II, but Wilhelm II won. Bismarck was fired.

Soon after, Germany lost Russia as an ally. Worse, Russia signed a treaty with France. Great Britain put aside its differences with France and strengthened their alliance. Russia, France and Great Britain together became the Triple Entente.

Under Wilhelm II, Germany's only ally among the major powers was Austria-Hungary.

When the Balkans flared and World War I started, Germany's alliance was the weaker alliance. [11]

World War I looked like this:

World War I

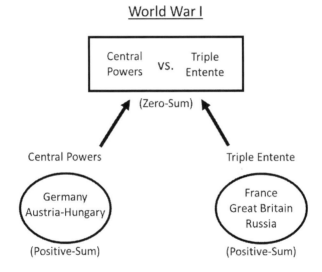

Strong alliances win wars.

Weak alliances lose wars.

To win a Zero-Sum Game, you need a strong Positive-Sum Game.

You need an alliance.

When Bin Laden declared war against the United States, he didn't have much of an alliance.

Bin Laden's alliance was jihadists from the Afghan war. Plus some young blood. A few rogue intelligence officers. Some shady financiers. And a reluctant Taliban.

Not much of an alliance.

Not much strength. Especially when you're going to war against the world's only superpower. And not just the world's only superpower. A superpower with an alliance of its own.

The U.S. had strong and close ties with British Commonwealth countries. Plus NATO. And other nations owed us favors. After 9/11, nearly the whole world was in the U.S. alliance against Bin Laden.

And ready to fight.

The "war on terror" looked like this:

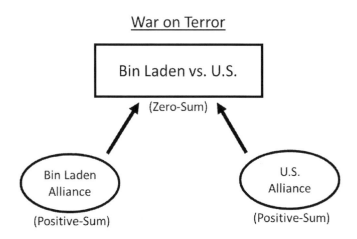

Which didn't make sense. Bin Laden had a weak alliance against the U.S.'s strong alliance. Bin Laden was sure to lose.

If that was Bin Laden's strategy, it didn't make sense. Why would Bin Laden start a war he was sure to lose?

To understand an enemy's strategy, you look forward through their eyes. As if you were in their situation. In their place. With their people. Surrounded by their things. And you look forward.

All the way to their Endgame.

To understand Bin Laden's strategy, you look to his Endgame. Further than the terrorist attacks in Africa and the Middle East. Further than 9/11. Further than his war with the United States.

You look all the way to Bin Laden's Endgame.

When you find it, you reason backward.

You see that for Bin Laden's strategy, attacking the United States made sense.

It was time to test Hypothesis #2 about the volunteer. The one about him being able to collect intelligence.

The test started simple. With a hypothetical.

What if we need X information? I asked. Can you get it?

"Why do you need to know that?" he asked.

Pushback.

Another bad sign.

It's just a hypothetical, I said.

A side test. Did he understand what "hypothetical" meant? With language barriers, spy to spy conversations sometimes drop to a six-year-old's level.

"Yes, yes. OK," he said.

He understood. Good.

But he wasn't happy about it. Like getting that kind of information was beneath him. Like it wasn't important enough. It wasn't tough guy enough, maybe.

Outstanding, I said. How will you get it?

He paused. "I can get it directly. No big deal."

What does directly mean? I asked.

He shrugged. "I see it and I get it."

Good, I said.

His brow narrowed. "But why do you need it? Can't you get it already?" he asked.

Pushback again. Both an alarming and a comforting thing. Alarming because it was the kind of thing a double-agent would ask. Now I had to think again about Hypothesis #1.

But the pushback was also comforting. Comforting because only a terrible double-agent would ask why I needed the information.

Then a third thing: maybe he had failed the side test. Maybe he hadn't understood what "hypothetical" meant. Maybe our conversations would be at a six-year-old's level after all.

A lot of red flags. Enough to signal a deeper problem: Our interests weren't aligned. Our strategies didn't meet. Maybe there was no Positive-Sum Game after all. No partnership. No win-win.

But it was still early. The red flags weren't the worst kinds of red flags. If you're a spy who walks away from every red flag, you don't do much. You don't get much intelligence. You don't meet many sources. You don't do your job.

So I stayed. I didn't walk away.

I gave him another chance.

I told him what to do before the next meeting. The things to bring me. Not hypotheticals. Real things to bring me.

Another chance. Another chance to prove his worth. So that I could justify the time with him. Time away from other important tasks. Other recruitments. Other intelligence collection.

I went over again the things to bring me.

He smiled and said he would.

In the 1930s, the Soviet Union had an espionage network in the United States. From breadth to depth to impact, it was maybe the most powerful espionage network in history.[12]

Soviet sources were at the highest levels of the U.S. Government. They gave Stalin advance warning of U.S. negotiating positions. They advised the Soviets on American weapons development. They were powerful enough to alter American foreign policy to benefit Soviet policy.

The Soviets built the espionage network by leveraging a simple fact: A lot of elite Americans in the 1930s sympathized with Communism.

A lot of elite Americans admired the Russian Revolution. They had lived through the Great

---

Depression. They had seen the benefits of the New Deal. To them, it seemed like capitalism was dying. It seemed like worldwide Communism was coming.

The proletariat would rise. Bourgeois capitalism would be defeated. A glorious future would be born. A Communist Revolution was coming.

If you believed that, you wanted to help your fellow Communists. You wanted to help the Soviets. And the U.S. didn't have much of a counterintelligence force. It was low risk for Americans to be spies for the Soviets in the 1930s.

If you had a high position in the U.S. government, the Soviets wanted you. So American Communists became spies for the Soviets. They became maybe the most powerful espionage network in history.

Until it fell apart.

It fell apart after two things happened.

The two things were:

>   1.   Stalin's Great Purge, and

>   2.   The Nazi-Soviet Non-Aggression Pact of 1939.[13]

At first glance, those two things shouldn't have

mattered.

Those two things happened far away from the United States. Far away from American Communists. Far away from Americans spying for the Soviets.

Yet, the effect was enormous.

Those two things caused American Communists to doubt their alliance with the Soviets.

In the Great Purge, Stalin killed fellow Communists. Hundreds of thousands. Maybe millions. It was a new phase of Stalin's rule. Where Stalin became a full-fledged dictator.

And then the Nazi-Soviet Non-Aggression Pact. A truce with fascists. A détente with the mortal enemies of Communism. A betrayal of the revolution, thought some American Communists.

American Communists started asking questions. Were the Soviets going to bring about the glorious Communist future, after all? Were the Soviets really Communist brothers and sisters after all? Were the Soviets the vanguard of the Communist Revolution? Or was the Soviet Union just another dictatorial state?

Some Americans decided to leave the Soviet spy network. Not everybody. But enough.

Whittaker Chambers was one. A former editor of *Time* magazine, he had been a courier for the Soviet spy network. Before he left the network, he hid documents that showed the extent of the Soviet espionage network in the U.S.

After World War II, Chambers dug out those documents. He delivered them to the FBI. Inside the documents were names of high-ranking American officials. They were identified as Soviet spies.

Testifying to Congress, Whittaker Chambers was called a liar. He was pilloried in the press. But material recovered from Soviet archives in the 1990s supported Chambers. American Communists had spied for the Soviets in the 1930s. The Soviet spy network had reached the highest levels of the U.S. government.

Then it died.

It died because some American Communists lost confidence in the Soviets. They lost their belief that the Soviets would be part of their Endgame of a Communist society.

If you were an American Communist in the 1930s, you wanted a Communist society. A global Communist society.

The Communist society would have three things:

---

1. People: The proletariat

2. Place: The whole world

3. Things: Resources produced by industry (and equitably divided)

In the imagination of the American Communists, there was nothing beyond a Communist society. Nothing past it. Nothing greater. Nothing more.

When a true Communist state came to be, it would be the end of history. There would be no more conflict. No more war. Everyone would live happily ever after. When a true Communist society came to be, no one would ever want to leave.

A Communist society was the Endgame.

When American Communists looked forward, a Communist society was the what they saw. When they reasoned backward, it made sense for them to join with the Soviets. To become spies for the Soviets. The Soviets were their allies in the revolution to come.

Until Stalin's Purges and Pact. Then, disillusionment. Questions.

Enough for some to turn on the Soviets.

Enough for some to choose new allies. Enough for

---

some, like Whittaker Chambers, to choose a new Endgame.[14]

Enough for the once-powerful Soviet espionage network in the United States to die.

An Endgame is the last game you can imagine.

It's when all conflicts are over. When all battles are won.

It's the happily ever after. The denouement in stories. The time of peace that comes after war.

Maybe, like Communists wanted, the Endgame happens on earth. It's an earthly paradise.

Or maybe the Endgame isn't on earth. Maybe it can't happen until heaven. Or in a different realm like Valhalla. Or in a spiritual paradise like Firdaws.

Or maybe the Endgame is now. For some people, their Endgame is not the future. It's not heaven. It's now. It's their family at a beach house with food and wine in the here and now. Their Endgame is now.

Whatever and whenever it is, every Endgame is a Positive-Sum Game.[15] Which means every Endgame has three things:

1. People

2. A place

3. Things to sustain it.

Because it's a Positive-Sum Game, an Endgame looks like this:

Endgame
(Positive-Sum)

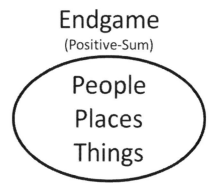

People
Places
Things

The Endgame is what you imagine to be your end. It's what you imagine when you look forward all the way to the end.

Which makes Endgames very important for strategy.

Because Endgames are what you reason backward from.

An Endgame is so important, you can't have a strategy without it.

For the American Communists in the 1930s, the Endgame looked like this:

Communist State
(Positive-Sum)

American Proletariat
North America
Resources

That was the Endgame they imagined. From there, they reasoned backward.

They reasoned backward and saw the proletariat was ruled by others. The proletariat lived in a capitalist society. Worse, the proletariat believed in religion. The proletariat was under the control of employers and pastors and priests.

For the Communist Society to exist, the Communists would need to somehow get those people, places and things. Without all three, their Endgame wouldn't exist.

Those who had the people, places and things the Communists wanted wouldn't give them up without a fight.

Which meant conflict was coming. Where the Communists would take those things from others.

There would be a Zero-Sum Game.

Reasoning backward, the future looked like this to the American Communists:

Communist State
(Positive-Sum)

American Proletariat
North America
Resources

People, Places,
and/or Things

Communists vs. Others

(Zero-Sum)

A Zero-Sum Game of Revolution would precede the

Positive-Sum Game of a Communist State.

Reasoning backward again, the Communists knew what all strategists know: The best way to win a Zero-Sum Game is to play a Positive-Sum Game. The best way to win a war is to have a strong alliance.

Which is why they built an alliance with the Soviets. Which is why they would spy for the Soviets.

The Soviets would help advance Communism in the United States. Win-win. Positive-Sum Game. An alliance.

Reasoning backward, the strategy of the American Communists looked like this:

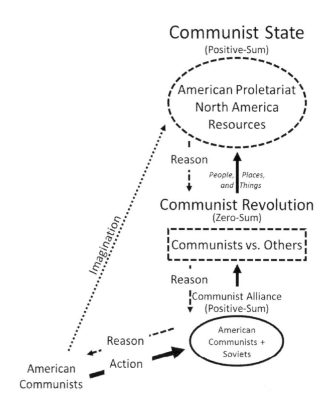

The American Communists had looked forward. They had reasoned backward.

They built a strategy.

A strategy that would start with a Positive-Sum alliance with the Soviets. So they could win the people,

---

places and things for their Endgame. Which was another Positive-Sum Game.

Most strategies follow the same pattern.

A Positive-Sum Game to win a Zero-Sum Game to get into an Endgame. Which is another Positive-Sum Game.

With imagination of the Endgame. Reasoning backward through the games. And then action to build an alliance, win a conflict and reach the Endgame.

It looks like this:

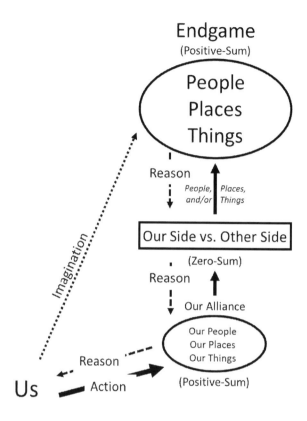

This strategic pattern is probably familiar because it's in a lot of stories.

This strategic pattern is in lots of books. Especially novels. Plus, it's how most movie plots go.

It's Luke and Han and Leia joining in an alliance. Their alliance fights against the Empire in a Zero-Sum Game. When they destroy the second Death Star, they win freedom for the people. They're celebrated by their allies. They've reached their Endgame.

It's Adrian and Paulie and Rocky Balboa. They build an alliance to defeat Apollo Creed in a Zero-Sum Game. After Rocky wins, it's Adrian he yells for. It's Paulie and Adrian he shares his victory with. They share his Endgame. Until it's time to fight again.

It's King Hrothgar and the Danes and Beowulf in an alliance. Against Grendel. Beowulf fights Grendel, wins and celebrates with the Danes in the mead hall. That's the Endgame. Until it's time to fight again.

But that's the strategy of just one side.

There's always another side.

There's always an antagonist.

There's always someone who wants the same people, places or things the protagonist wants.

There's always an enemy.

An enemy with a strategy of their own. An Endgame of their own. An alliance of their own, too.

Only one side will win.

When you put the two strategies together, it looks like this:

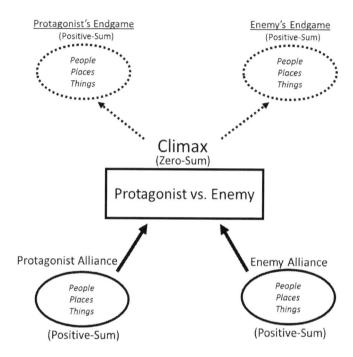

The protagonist builds an alliance to defeat the enemy. The enemy builds an alliance to defeat the protagonist.

They come together in a conflict. A climax. Where only one side can win.

Which means only one Endgame can exist.

Positive-Sum, then Zero-Sum, then Positive-Sum again. Games arranged in the most efficient way to get the protagonist to their Endgame.

When you see the pattern, you see it everywhere.

You see it in wars.

You see it in politics.

You see it in business.

You even see it in families.

You see people working to get to their Endgame. You see them building alliances to win conflicts. You see the result of conflicts is one side wins people, places and/or things. You see people building strategies to reach their Endgame.

And then they act. They act to create and win the games that get them to their Endgame.

To understand someone else's strategy, you look for their Endgame. And then you reason backward.

If you do it right, you see the Zero-Sum Games they

will play. You see who their enemies will be.

And you see the Positive-Sum alliances they must build to defeat their enemies.

Put the games together, and you see their strategy.

You see that everyone is building strategies to get to their Endgame.

When he fought in Afghanistan in the 1970s, Bin Laden hid his Endgame.

He didn't publicize his Endgame. He didn't issue fatwas and video recordings. He didn't talk about the people, places and things he wanted in it. Bin Laden kept his Endgame hidden.

Which is why he was part of the U.S.-Afghan alliance in the Soviet-Afghan War.

On the other side was the Soviet's alliance.

The alliances and the conflict looked like this:

Out of that war would come one of two Endgames:

Endgame A: Afghanistan under Afghan rule, with the people of Afghanistan, the land of Afghanistan and the resources of Afghanistan; or

Endgame B: Afghanistan under Soviet occupation, with the Soviets ruling over the people of Afghanistan, the land of Afghanistan and the resources of Afghanistan.

With the two possible Endgames included, it looked like this:

One of those two Endgames would exist at the end of the war. One side would have the land and people and resources of Afghanistan. The other would not.

Eventually, the U.S.-Afghan Alliance won. The Soviets withdrew. Afghanistan was ruled by Afghans. Which meant Endgame A existed.[16]

Bin Laden was part of the winning alliance. He had contributed. He had fought. He had helped defeat the Soviet enemy. He had helped Endgame A come to be.

But Endgame A wasn't Bin Laden's Endgame.

Bin Laden had a bigger Endgame in mind.

To get there, Bin Laden needed an alliance.

Bin Laden used the Soviet-Afghan War as a proving ground for his alliance. He used it to evaluate people. To judge fighters. He used it to build a network of people who believed what he believed. People he could trust.

Bin Laden created a list of those people. In Bin Laden's mind, the list was a database. A database of trusted people. A database of fighters. Which is why he called it "The Base." In Arabic, "The Base" is "Al-Qaeda."

At first, Al-Qaeda was a loose alliance. But it was a building block for the games to come. A first step to Bin Laden's Endgame.

When Saddam Hussein got belligerent in the early 1990's, Bin Laden saw an opportunity. He offered Al-Qaeda to the Saudis as protection.

Bin Laden had every reason to think the Saudis would accept his offer. Bin Laden, though ethnic Yemeni, had Saudi citizenship. Bin Laden's father had made billions building things for the Saudis. Bin Laden knew many Saudi royals. And they were fellow Muslims.

But the Saudis told Bin Laden no.

The Saudis took an American offer of protection instead. The offer meant the Saudis would host more American troops on Saudi soil. It meant expanding American military bases in Saudi Arabia.

It meant Bin Laden was excluded. It meant Bin Laden's fighters were rejected. It meant the Saudis chose American infidels over Bin Laden.

Which hurt Bin Laden. In a big way.

After Saddam Hussein was contained, Bin Laden acted out. He railed against the Saudis and was banished in 1992. He went to East Africa, where he caused more trouble. The Saudis revoked Bin Laden's citizenship. Then, they froze his assets.

Cut off, Bin Laden went back to Afghanistan. There, he had time to think. He had time to fully imagine his Endgame. He had time to reason backward. He had time to build a strategy.

Then, it was time for Bin Laden to act.

Bin Laden's first step: Build his alliance.

Bin Laden gave speeches. He did interviews. He published videos and pamphlets. He did everything he could to attract like-minded people to his cause.

Most importantly, Bin Laden started talking about his

Endgame.

Bin Laden said he was going to build a Caliphate.

Bin Laden's Caliphate would have people, places and things, just like every Endgame:

1. People: Muslim believers, otherwise known as the "Ummah."

2. Place: The Middle East, especially the "Holy Places" of Mecca and Jerusalem.

3. Things: Resources to sustain the Ummah.

In the 1990s, Bin Laden had none of those.

He had none of the Ummah under his rule. He had very little in the way of resources. And he wasn't even in the Middle East. He was in Afghanistan with just a small following and few resources.

In the 1990s, Bin Laden was far from a Caliphate in every possible way.

But Bin Laden built a strategy anyway. He built it by reasoning backward.

When Bin Laden reasoned backward, the world looked like this:

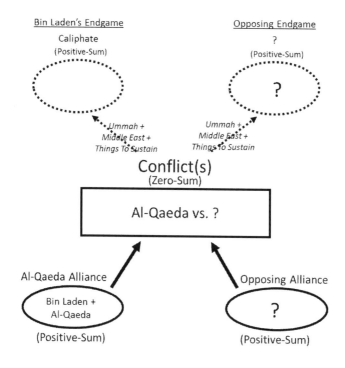

Bin Laden looked at what he needed for a Caliphate: The Ummah. The "Holy Places." And things to sustain it.

Then, he reasoned backward. To whom he would fight for them. To whom he would have a conflict with.

And then, reasoned backward again.

To who was on the other side. To who was in the opposing alliance. To who would resist him taking the Ummah, the Middle East and its resources.

Bin Laden filled in the blanks. He identified allies, enemies, and enemies' alliances. Then, it was time to act.

It was time to strengthen his allies. It was time to weaken his enemies. And, most significantly, it was time to weaken his enemies' allies.

But Bin Laden wanted something else.

Something that touches on another dimension of strategy.

It's a dimension of strategy sometimes more important than Positive-Sum and Zero-Sum Games. A dimension that forced Bin Laden to take greater risks. A dimension that drove many of Bin Laden's decisions.

A dimension embedded in Bin Laden's Endgame.

Because Bin Laden didn't want just any Caliphate.

Bin Laden wanted a Caliphate where he was Caliph.

Caliph means successor of Mohammed. Leader of the Caliphate.

The Boss.

Bin Laden wanted to be the boss. The leader. The Caliph.

Which meant he would need to win a different type of game.

Bin Laden wanted to win a game within the Caliphate.

Bin Laden would need to win a game within his Endgame.

Bin Laden would need to win a Boss Game.

Bin Laden didn't only build a strategy for a Caliphate.

He also built a strategy to become Caliph.

Spies in movies usually want one thing.

One document. One code. One briefcase.

One objective.

One thing. [17]

Which is fun, if you're in the audience.

Will the spy get the one thing or not? Will they fail or

succeed? Will they win or lose? Will they get it or not? Going after one thing creates tension. Going after one thing forces desperate moves. Going after one thing creates crises. Going after one thing makes a movie entertaining.

But if you're a real spy, you're not an entertainer. Which means you don't go after one thing.

You avoid crises. You avoid desperate moves. Because too many desperate moves and crises means you're arrested. Or worse.

You never go after one thing.

Never one document. Never one code. Never one briefcase.

Never one objective.

Never one thing.

You want more than one thing.

You want all the things that advance your strategy.

Which is lots of things.

Lots of documents. Lots of codes. Lots of briefcases.

Which also means lots of ways to win. Lots of pathways to success. If you can't get one thing, you get something else. If you didn't get something today, you get it tomorrow.

When it comes to telling a source what to bring you, you follow the same pattern. You never ask for one document. Or one code. Or one briefcase. Never a single objective.

Because you don't want the source to make desperate moves. You don't want to create crises. You want the source to succeed.

Plus, telling a source to bring you lots of things helps in two other ways:

1. It forces the source to make choices.

2. It allows you to mix real espionage requirements with fake ones.

Which means you can judge the source's choices. And you can hide what you know and don't know, in case they're a double-agent.

In the third meeting with the lying source, I started there.

I asked what he got.

He smiled. Bright and toothy with success.

"It wasn't easy," he said.

He pushed a torn-up scrap of paper across the table.

I didn't care that it was a torn-up scrap of paper. I had seen worse. Used worse. At least there were no blood stains.

Why is it on a torn-up scrap of paper? I asked.

"It's what I had when my friend called back with the information," he said.

A problem. A problem because he had implied he had direct access to documents. Lots of documents. Original documents. Not a transcription of a phone call on a torn-up scrap of paper.

I clarified.

You didn't see the original document?

"No," he said. "My friend saw it. He told me what it said."

Which was bad. A friend was bad.

A friend was bad because it meant the source had asked the friend a direct question. Now, the friend knew what he'd asked for. What he wanted.

But at least he didn't tell the friend about me. Or did he?

I asked.

"No," he said, shaking his head. "Of course not. I told him it was something I needed for something else I was working on."

Who's the friend? I asked.

He paused. His hands grabbed each other. His fingers threaded and his thumbs twiddled.

He didn't want to tell me. Which was good. Which meant the friend was probably real. He would tell me eventually, but it was good that he didn't want to. It was good that he wanted to protect his friend.

And I had bigger concerns.

I thought he had direct access to documents. I thought there were no go-betweens. I thought he could get a document and give it to me.

But he had gone to a friend.

Then there was his choices. I had given him lots of things to get. Lots of ways to win. If this was the one he chose, it meant the others weren't likely.

Which meant his capability was limited.

Which meant I had to decide. Either:

1. Go forward, which would mean more work, more time and more effort; or

2. End it there.

I chose Option 1.

I chose Option 1 because he wasn't the first source to start out this way. When people first learn the ways of real spies, there's an adjustment. They need to forget a lot of what they think they know about espionage. They need to learn new things.

Other sources who had started this way had gone on to great things. They got a job change or new access to important intelligence. They had produced great things. A lot of great things.

So I chose Option 1. I decided to put the work and time and effort in.

I made a deal with the lying source.

He joined our alliance.

I confirmed again that our relationship was secret. That he hadn't told anyone. That we were in this together.

"Of course," he said. "What are we going to do now?"

We're going to do more like what we've done, I told

him.

I gave him lots of things to do. But not the most important things.

I held back. To be sure that he would be careful. To be sure he could get to a meeting without being followed. To be sure his choices were good. To be sure he wasn't a double-agent. I didn't think he was, but that was just a hypothesis.

Over the next several meetings, I tested more hypotheses. I designed ways to know if he was helpful. If he was worth the time. He didn't pass all of them, but he passed enough.

Then came an opportunity for something bigger.

An opportunity to join a bigger team. A team that did important work.

Joining the team meant others would be exposed to him.

Before that, we'd have to be absolutely sure he was good. That he was on our side. That we could trust him with lives. Our lives.

That's when we discovered the lie.

7

The Other Side's Strategy

"If you know yourself but not the other side, for every victory gained you will also suffer a defeat." – Sun Tzu

I took the lying source to a nice Midwestern city in the United States. Not the most impressive city in the United States. Not the largest city. Not the most beautiful city. A nice city with nice people.

The nice people in the nice city like to ask where you're from. If you say you're from overseas, they ask how you like America. They talk about if they've been to your country. They're friendly. Open. Generous. They're great for a source to meet.

Great because sources are working for them, ultimately. If a source is working with the CIA, they're working for people of the United States. Friendly, generous and open people like these.

Midwestern cities are good for another reason: It's easy to pick out surveillants. It's easy to see who doesn't belong. This one had plenty of deserted side streets. And elevation changes. Easy to see if you're being followed.

I didn't think I'd be surveilled in a Midwestern city. But that was just a hypothesis. To be tested.

So I tested it. And went to meet the source.

He hadn't been followed, he said. He was certain, he said. Which he shouldn't have been. It was just a hypothesis.

I told the source the agenda: We would meet a colleague of mine. The colleague would ask questions. It was important to answer honestly. It was important to be truthful.

"You can trust me," he said.

We met in a suite. My colleague took him into one room and closed the door. I sat in the adjoining room and turned on the TV.

When you've been outside the United States for a while, there's always something new when you return.

This time it was poker in primetime on ESPN, which was strange. I thought ESPN only did sports. But then it made sense: Poker was a Zero-Sum Game. Like sports. If you like to watch sports for the strategy and tension and competition, poker gives you the same thing. With less athleticism.

So I watched poker. You could see everybody's cards in real time. You could see how each player played. You could analyze each player's tactics in the Zero-Sum Game. Strategy, tension and competition.

I watched poker for an hour.

Then I heard a yell.

I got to the door. Put a hand on it. Listened.

It was my colleague yelling. Not in pain. Not in surprise.

He was yelling in anger.

Which was ok. Expected. I stepped back. Stood and listened for another minute. Then, the yelling stopped.

Back to poker. I watched another hour. Then there was a baseball game.

Finally, my colleague came out. Just him. He closed the door softly behind him.

Pity on his face. Like he was sorry. Sorry to tell me what he had to tell me.

"He's been lying."

I didn't want to ask the next question.

Lying about what? I asked.

My colleague took a deep breath. "Lying about who he told about you."

My first thought was double-agent. Second and third and fourth thoughts were the things I'd have to clean up. The lines I'd have to cut. The backfilling I'd have to do overseas.

Who did he tell? I asked.

"Six people," said my colleague. "His father and five friends. None intel, as far as he knows."

None intel? I confirmed.

"None intel, as far as he knows."

Not a double-agent, then.

But six people.

Six people is a lot.

Six people could tell six other people. And six other people could tell six others. One of whom could be intel. Someone who would do something about me.

My colleague went back in. I started planning how to clean up the mess. No more poker for me.

An hour later, my colleague came out again. "Now, it's 18. He told 18 people about you and the CIA."

By the end of the day, it was 23. He told 23 people that he was working with the CIA. With me.

Twenty-three.

A ridiculous number. That would be practically everyone he knows.

Did it start after our second meeting? When he got the information on the torn scrap of paper? Had he told that friend why he wanted the information? That he was going to give it to the CIA?

Maybe it was earlier. Maybe he told his friends at the very beginning. Before our first meeting. Maybe the guy who couldn't place me in the restaurant was his friend, after all.

Didn't matter.

To be safe, I assumed it started at the beginning.

And I saw my mistake: I assumed the wrong Endgame for the lying source. I thought his Endgame was one thing, when it was another.

_____

I had assumed he wanted to help in the fight against terrorism, when it was something else.

Now, his lies exposed his Endgame. Now, I saw the people, places and things in his Endgame.

And there was something else. Another wrinkle. Another dimension to the lying source's Endgame.

Which was the real reason he exposed me to 23 people.

It was the game inside his Endgame.

In the winter of 2011, protests flashed across the Arab world. It started with a self-immolation in Tunisia. It burned east to the Sultanates. It raged west to Libya.

Overnight, tanks and machine guns and concrete barriers appeared in city squares. Protesters massed. Riot police took position.

There were clashes. Then there were stalemates. Then there were talks. Then more clashes. More stalemates.

As winter warmed to spring, the protests got a name: The Arab Spring.

From the outside, it looked like a revolution in slow-motion. The protesters lost in some places. They won in others. In some places, they lost, then won, then lost again.

From the outside, it looked like a simple Zero-Sum Game.

Protesters vs. Arab leaders.

If one side won power, the other lost it. Zero-Sum.

On the inside, it was different.

On the inside, you saw people hold back.

When someone thinks about playing a Zero-Sum Game, they don't only think about winning. They also think about losing. They think about what happens if they lose. They think about what the winner will do to them if they lose.

Which is one of three things.

After a Zero-Sum Game, there are three things that can happen between the winner and loser:

1. The loser is killed, vanquished or runs away, which means the winner and loser never interact again (No

Future Games)

2. The loser and winner engage in another Zero-Sum Game (Future Zero-Sum Games)[18]

3. The loser and winner's next interaction is a Positive-Sum Game. They shift from enemies to allies. The loser and winner work together. (Future Positive-Sum Games)

From the outside, the Arab Spring looked like the first type of Zero-Sum Game. The losers would be vanquished. They would be killed or exiled. The Arab Spring looked like first type of Zero-Sum Game.

Or maybe the second type of Zero-Sum Game. An interminable civil war. Zero-Sum Game after Zero-Sum Game. Conflict after conflict. One side against the other forever.

But if you were inside the Arab Spring, you saw something different.

You saw that most people wanted to play the third type of Zero-Sum Game.

If you were an Egyptian protester, you didn't like the 30-year-old state of emergency laws. You didn't like the lack of free speech. You didn't like that you had a PhD but could only get a job giving tours. You didn't like how food was distributed. You didn't like a lot of things.

But there were other things you liked about Egypt. Maybe you liked how the Egyptian government protected you from Israelis. And from Tunisians. And from Libyans. Maybe you liked that the Egyptian government subsidized your education. Maybe you liked that the Egyptian government gave some food to your family.

But maybe you didn't like that a neighbor got more. Or had a better job. Or got more vacation time than you did. Or maybe you experienced an injustice. When the Egyptian government punished you or a family member without reason.

So you protested. You protested so good people would get justice. So the right things would be done.

But you didn't want to destroy Egypt. You didn't want to destroy even the government of Egypt. You just wanted different decisions made. You wanted someone else in charge. You wanted a better boss.

Which meant you held back. You didn't want too much violence. You didn't want things to get out of control. You didn't want the clashes to become the second type of Zero-Sum Game. You didn't want a civil war. And you didn't want the first type of result from the protests. You didn't want the winner to destroy the loser.

You wanted the third type of Zero-Sum Game. You wanted a Positive-Sum Game to be the next game played. You wanted peace and cooperation in the end. You wanted Egypt to stay Egypt. You wanted the nation to stay together.

You just wanted a different kind of boss.

A better kind of boss.

Inside every Positive-Sum Game, some people have more power than others. Some people make more important decisions than others. Some people decide what the rest of the group will do. Inside every Positive-Sum Game, someone is the boss.

Sometimes, the boss is a committee. Sometimes, it's a group within the larger group. But every committee has a chairman. Every group has a leader. Which means one person is usually the ultimate boss. Usually, one person makes decisions for a group.

Usually, groups have a hierarchy of decision-making.

It looks like this:

Few at the top. Often, just one. Many more below.

A hierarchy.

But hierarchies don't exist in isolation.

Hierarchies exist inside a larger game. Usually, hierarchies exist when people agree to follow the boss's decisions.

It's not always voluntary. Sometimes, there are tapestries of threats to keep underlings in line. Punishments keep the people at the bottom following the decisions of people at the top. It's how dictatorships are run.

But fortunately, dictatorships are rare.

Usually, hierarchies exist inside a Positive-Sum Game. Where underlings voluntarily follow the decisions of people at the top. Because everyone benefits. Because it's a win-win.

When you put a hierarchy inside a Positive-Sum Game with the people, places and things every Positive-Sum Game requires, it looks like this:

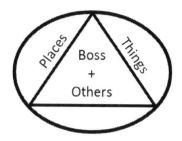

If you were in Egypt before the Arab Spring, Egypt looked like this:

Egypt Pre-Arab Spring

If you were an Egyptian protester, you didn't want Mubarrak at the top. You wanted someone different. You wanted a different hierarchy inside Egypt. You wanted a different boss. You wanted someone else making decisions. You wanted Mubarrak out.

But you didn't want to destroy the larger Positive-Sum Game. You didn't want to lose the people, places or things of Egypt. You just wanted to change the hierarchy inside it.

You wanted Egypt to stay Egypt. You wanted Egypt to keep all its resources. You wanted the Positive-Sum Game to continue. Just with different decisions made. Just with a different hierarchy inside it.

You wanted this:

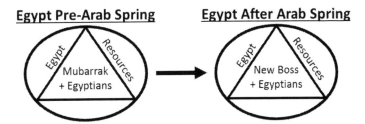

You probably wanted the hierarchy to be chosen differently, too. By a vote, maybe. Or based on ethnicity. Or maybe you wanted an Islamic cleric to have ultimate authority for Egypt.

Whoever you wanted to be the new boss, you didn't want to destroy Egypt. You wanted to stay joined to the people, places and things of Egypt. You didn't want to destroy the Positive-Sum Game.

You wanted Egypt to stay Egypt.

Which meant when the protests started, you held back.

You avoided bloodshed. You didn't throw as many rocks as you could have. You didn't shoot as many rockets as you could have. You didn't kill as many policemen as you could have.

But sometimes, events spiral out of control. Sometimes, there's a misunderstanding or a bad interpretation of an order or a lack of compromise.

Sometimes a Boss Game becomes one of the first two types of Zero-Sum Game. A Civil war. Or a genocide.

Informal rules change. Inhibitions are lost. No one holds back.

Strong men take charge. People disappear. It only ends when one side gains complete and total victory. Or the country fractures into pieces.

Fortunately, those events are rare.

Usually, Boss Games end peacefully. Usually, people compromise. Usually, leaders negotiate.

Which means protesters become part of the government. Everyone agrees on a new set of rules. Everyone agrees to follow the decisions of the new boss, however the new boss is chosen.

Which is what happened in most countries after the Arab Spring. Mubarrak left Egypt, but Egyptians stayed Egyptian. Ben Ali left Tunisia, but Tunisians stayed Tunisian. A Positive-Sum Game followed.

But it didn't happen everywhere.

Libya fractured. Libya became the 2nd type of Zero-Sum Game. The one where people keep fighting. Where Zero-Sum Game follows Zero-Sum Game. Civil war.

Which is why spies watch for Boss Games. Not only for what they are and who wins. Also for what they can become. For the games that will follow.

Because what starts off as a Boss Game can become a revolution. Or a civil war. Or a genocide.

You watch for Boss Games. And you watch for Boss games spiraling out of control. Because they can turn into something much worse.

When you're looking at the other side's strategy, you watch Boss Games closely. You watch because if the boss of the other side changes, their strategy will change, too. An ally can become an enemy.

But if the other side is already an enemy, there's another reason to watch Boss Games closely.

If the other side is an enemy, their boss will build a

strategy to make sure they stay boss.

Which may mean attacking you.

Bin Laden had won the Boss Game inside Al-Qaeda. Which seemed inevitable. After all, Bin Laden had created Al-Qaeda. It was his database of trusted fighters.

But that didn't mean Al-Qaeda would stay his. There was a chance someone else could take over. Someone more charismatic. Or stronger. Or more devout. There was competition inside Al-Qaeda to be boss, as there is in any group.

But Bin Laden stayed boss. Bin Laden was the boss of Al-Qaeda.

Al-Qaeda looked like this:

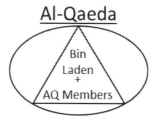

Which meant Bin Laden made the important decisions for Al-Qaeda. He set the strategic direction for the group.

When we put a hierarchy inside Al-Qaeda, Bin Laden's strategy looks like this:

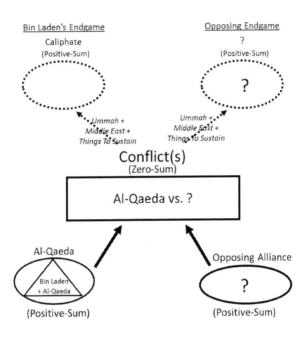

Being boss of Al-Qaeda was important to Bin Laden.

But he wanted much more than that.

Bin Laden wanted to be Caliph.

Bin Laden wanted to be boss in the Caliphate to come.

When he won, Bin Laden imagined he would be the true successor to Mohammed. He would be the spiritual and political leader of the Ummah. Which is why Bin Laden consciously mimicked Mohammed in everything he did.

Bin Laden imagined a Caliphate that looked like this:

The Caliphate

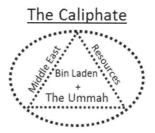

Bin Laden would be Caliph. He would rule over the Ummah in the Middle East and use its resources to sustain the Caliphate.

Putting that hierarchy into Bin Laden's Endgame, Bin Laden's strategy looked like this:

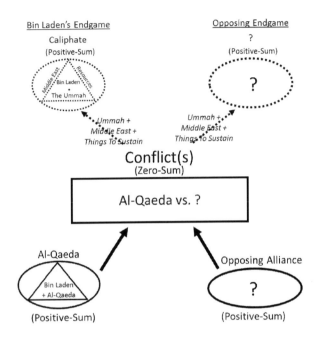

In early 2001, Bin Laden was a long way from his Endgame. A long way from becoming Caliph.

And Bin Laden had another problem. A strategic problem.

The people, places and things Bin Laden needed for a Caliphate were under the rule of fellow Muslims.

The Ummah would frown on attacking fellow Muslims. Some of the Ummah might even say Bin Laden could never be Caliph if he attacked fellow Muslims.

But Bin Laden couldn't sit back. He couldn't accept the status quo.

To change it, Bin Laden needed a conflict. He needed to attack someone. He needed to start a war. Or else his Endgame would never come to be. He would never become Caliph.

If he couldn't attack Muslims, who could Bin Laden attack?

Attacking Russia would be of limited value.

Attacking Israel was too hard.

Attacking India wouldn't prove anything.

Attacking Europe wouldn't get him anything.

So Bin Laden chose to attack the United States.

But Bin Laden didn't just attack the United States because he wanted to start a war. There were other strategic reasons why he chose to attack the U.S.

Strategic reasons that started with the fact there was an Endgame that stood as a rival to his Caliphate.

An Endgame that had the United States as its boss.

To become President of the United States, you win a lot of Boss Games. First were state-level primaries. Then the general election, with many games inside it. Then the Electoral College.

If you're President, you won all those games.

You're boss of the richest, most powerful country in the world.

At first, it feels like this:

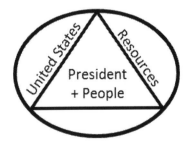

You take office by swearing an oath to the Constitution of United States. The Constitution lays out which decisions you can make. Which decisions Congress and the Supreme Court will make. Which decisions the states and individuals will make. Which decisions you'll need others to agree to for new laws.

You get started in the first 100 days. You focus on your signature issue. The one you campaigned on. The one people elected you to do. The one you said you'd get done the first year. You get to work.

You work with Congress. The House and Senate. You twist arms and negotiate. Which means a lot of compromising. Which means accepting some changes from your original plan.

You work and work. Maybe you fail. Maybe your first year is a disaster.

Or maybe you succeed. Congress passes a law that's not what you wanted. But maybe it's close. Close enough. So you sign it and make it a law.

Then, it's challenged in court. And appealed to the Supreme Court. Where it's determined to be Constitutional. Or not. Or changed again by interpretation.

If you succeed, you got something close to what you

wanted. But not exactly what you wanted.

The process was exhausting. You burned political capital. You made a lot of promises. Some of those promises will take the rest of your Presidency to deliver. And you didn't get exactly what you wanted.

You recognize a simple fact: Presidential decision-making is limited. Being boss in a constitutional system like the United States is limiting.

The Constitution limits your power. Congress limits your power. The opposing party limits your power. The Supreme Court limits your power. Your decisions rarely turn into action. And even more rarely, into results.

Plus, you have mid-term elections. Where the American people will vote by proxy on your decisions. Up or down. And after your first term is done, the American people can vote again. They can keep you or replace you. They can elect someone who undoes everything you did. Or doesn't.

The Boss Game in the United States looks more like this:

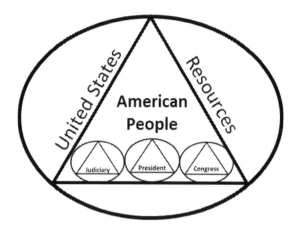

At least, that's true for decisions you make about what happens within the borders of the United States.

For decisions on what happens outside U.S. borders, it's different.

Outside the United States, the Constitution gives the President more power. Congress doesn't intervene as much. The opposing party gives you more latitude. The Supreme Court only steps in if something crazy happens. Outside the United States, it's a lot easier to turn your decisions into action. And into results.

Outside the United States you are Commander-in-

Chief. You have more power. On a bigger playing field.

Which is why most Presidencies follow a pattern. At the beginning, the President focuses on domestic issues. Then the President conflicts with Congress. And the Supreme Court. And takes some losses. Domestically, the President is not as powerful as they want to be.

Outside the United States, international institutions are less likely to stand in an American President's way. Foreign countries may resist, but that's a different kind of game. Played with tools not available domestically. Like the U.S. Armed Forces. And the CIA.

Which creates a natural dynamic: Presidents start making decisions where their decisions are turned into action. Where they can get results. Which is outside U.S. borders.

As a Presidency goes on, Presidents are more likely to spend time on international issues.[19]

Presidents create currency agreements, world trade agreements and international institutions. They create a network of defense alliances and support. A world system under U.S. rules.

Most other countries don't mind. They see the benefit of working within the U.S.-led system. Most countries have joined a U.S. defense treaty or trade agreement. Most countries are in a Positive-Sum Game with the United States. Win-win for everyone.

Add it all together, and it's one big Positive-Sum Game.

Some call the global Positive-Sum Game the post-Cold War system. But that defines it by what it's not. Some call it Western Civilization. But includes Asia, too. Some call it the New World Order. But that's creepy.

Most of the time, a Positive-Sum Game takes its name from its leader. Like law firms have top partners in their names. Like Walmart was named for Sam Walton. Like kingdoms are named for kings. Caliphates for caliphs. Like how the Pax Romana was named for Rome.

Some people call it the Pax Americana.

If that's what we call it, the Pax Americana looks like this:

Pax Americana

Like every Positive-Sum Game, it has people (most people in the world), places (most places in the world) and things (most resources in the world).

But not everyone likes it.

Some people don't like U.S. leadership. Some people don't like U.S. rules or institutions or dispute mechanisms. Some people don't like U.S. Presidents. Some people want more from the Pax Americana. They're not winning as much as they'd like in the Pax Americana.

So they start a conflict. Maybe it's the third type of

Zero-Sum Game against the United States: They want to win the power to make certain decisions.

But they hold back. They limit the conflict to a vote at the U.N. Or a proxy war in a remote corner of the world. They don't take the conflict too far. They don't want to destroy the world system.

But some don't see any benefit to the Pax Americana. They want it destroyed. They want to break the world into pieces. Into regions. Maybe they want a Pax Sinica. Or a Pax Africanus. They want to start wars. The kind of wars where the losers are vanquished or killed. They want the first type of Zero-Sum Game.

Which are threats.

When you're an American spy, it's your job to watch for those threats.

Because it's always easier to win a Zero-Sum Game before it starts.

When you're an American spy, you're preparing for the next war. You're watching potential enemies. You're helping allies. You're getting your Positive-Sum Games and Zero-Sum Games in line. To get to your Endgame.

You're reasoning backward. From the Pax Americana. To the conflicts that threaten it. To the alliances that support it.

When you're a spy, you're building micro-strategies to win. You're building alliances to win the conflicts that will come.

You're using that strategy to prioritize which intelligence is important. And what's not necessary. Which sources to work with. And which aren't worth the time. Which relationships are worth the risk and denied area travel and high-threat encounters. And which aren't.

You're reasoning backward to today. To which meetings are worth the risk. And which aren't.

Which is important when your boss tells you to do something you shouldn't.

I hadn't seen the lying source's strategy. Because I hadn't seen his Endgame.

I hadn't seen it because I made a mistake. A mistake I had made before. A mistake I didn't make again.

My mistake was that I believed his Endgame was

similar to mine. But it wasn't. He didn't care about saving lives. Or fighting terrorism. Or the Pax Americana.

He just cared about his friends. His village. And his influence in it.

He cared about a very small Boss Game.

I hadn't seen that the lying source had this Endgame:

All he cared about what his village and his influence in it.

This type of Endgame isn't unusual. It isn't unusual for people to want to be a leader among their friends. It isn't unusual to want to impress the people around them. It isn't unusual to want to be popular and deferred to and respected. It isn't unusual to want to be the boss.

But it was the first time I'd seen it up close in espionage.

It was the first time I'd seen it drive such an obviously dangerous strategy. It was the first time I'd seen it mean a cavalier attitude toward secrecy. It was the first time I'd seen it mean stupidity and risk.

All to impress his friends.

Looking back, there were clues in our first conversation. When he talked about gun battles. When he acted like a tough guy.

He was trying to impress.

Which hadn't worked with me. I had tried to diminish what he thought were his impressive skills. His tough guy skills. I had tried to make him more like a spy.

Which maybe he didn't like.

When I turned him toward intelligence collection rather than tough guy activities, he turned on me. He leveraged me. He took what I gave him and shared it with others.

He took without giving.

He turned our relationship into a Zero-Sum Game.

His strategy had become this:

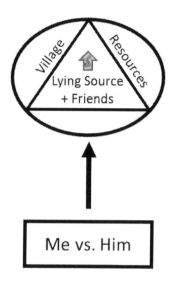

He took information. He took knowledge. He took whatever would push him higher in his Boss Game. He took things.

But he hadn't taken that much.

Because I had held back. I had waited to talk about the important things. If the onion of intelligence collection has twenty layers, he had barely been past the first.

But he didn't know that.

He didn't know there was much more.

He didn't know that his stupid strategy had stopped him from something much bigger.

Now, he would never know.

Now, it was over.

Now, it was time to deal with him.

But there were risks.

Risks because he knew he had been caught. He knew that I knew.

Which meant he was thinking about what I would do next. He was thinking about whether I would do bad things.

He was thinking of worst-case scenarios.

Worst-case scenarios that came from spy movies. From what spies in the movies would do. James Bond. Jason Bourne. Jack Bauer.

Movie spies hurt people. Sometimes, movie spies kill people. Sometimes, movie spies blow up whole villages. For less than what he'd done.

Now, he was gaming out what I would do. Would I

hurt him? Worse: Kill him? Worse still: Hurt his family?

I wouldn't. But he didn't know that.

Which was a problem.

A strategic problem.

Before 9/11, we knew Bin Laden was a threat to U.S. interests abroad. He attacked us in Africa. He attacked us in the Middle East. He had the capability and the will to attack U.S. interests abroad.

We knew Bin Laden wanted a Caliphate. We knew he wanted to be Caliph. We knew he wanted the Ummah, the Middle East and its resources under his rule.

But few saw that Bin Laden's strategy was a threat to the United States homeland.

Few reasoned backward from Bin Laden's Endgame to his full strategy. Few reasoned backward to how Bin Laden could win the people, places and things for a Caliphate. Few reasoned backward to Bin Laden attacking the U.S. homeland.

The first step backward for Bin Laden from a Caliphate was a Zero-Sum Game. A Zero-Sum Game against those who had the people, places and things Bin Laden needed for a Caliphate: Arab Rulers.

Isolated, it looked like this:

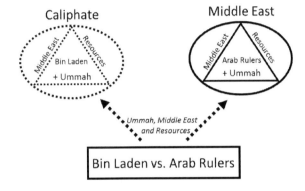

Eventually, there would be a conflict between Bin Laden and the Arab Rulers.

If Bin Laden won, there would be a Caliphate. If Arab Rulers won, there would be the status quo.

Then, the next step backward. To the alliances that would fight this conflict.

Bin Laden saw that the Arab Rulers were part of an alliance. An American-led alliance.

Which Bin Laden saw first-hand before the First Gulf War. That's when Arab Rulers rejected Bin Laden's offer of help. That's when Bin Laden saw the Middle East was embedded in the Pax Americana.

When Bin Laden saw that, he looked at the bigger picture.

Bin Laden saw this:

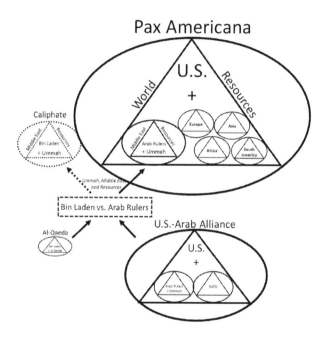

Bin Laden saw that to build a Caliphate, he would

need to weaken the Arab Rulers. Which he could do by weakening their alliance. By pulling them away from the Pax Americana. Bin Laden wanted to separate Arab Rulers from the United States.

After separating Arab Rulers from the United States, he would defeat them individually. Which would be easier. Maybe, without force. Bin Laden could use his position as a cleric to persuade the Ummah to overthrow the Arab Rulers.

It wasn't a new strategy. A similar strategy had worked in Afghanistan. There, a dominating foreign state had been terrorized into withdrawing. When the foreign state was gone, theocratic warlords fought for power.

In Afghanistan, that's how the Taliban had won.

Bin Laden wanted what happened in Afghanistan to happen in the Middle East.

Bin Laden wanted the world to look like this:

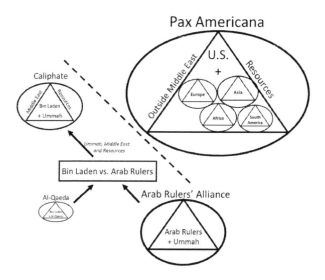

Bin Laden wanted to cut the Middle East away from the rest of the world.

Bin Laden wanted the Middle East to leave the Pax Americana. To become a separate entity. So that he could fight the Arab Rulers directly. A fight Bin Laden thought he could win.

With that strategy in mind, Bin Laden launched the attacks on 9/11.

And he used Saudi passport holders to do it.

There's no better way to destroy an alliance than to have one side of the alliance attack the other. There's no better way to sow distrust. There's no better way to weaken. There's no better way to create fear in one side and anger in the other.

In the hours after 9/11, the Saudis felt that fear. They gathered as many of their citizens as they could. When the airports reopened, the Saudis took them on private planes back to Saudi Arabia.

The Saudis were right to be worried. Some Americans blamed the Saudis for 9/11. Some Americans wanted the U.S. alliance with the Saudis to stop. Some Americans wanted to stop supporting Arab Rulers. Some wanted to withdraw completely from the Middle East.

The U.S.-Arab Rulers' alliance was weakened on 9/11.

Just as Bin Laden wanted.

The attacks on 9/11 did four things to weaken Bin Laden's enemies. And the attacks did four things to strengthen Bin Laden.

How Bin Laden strengthened himself on 9/11:

1. Bin Laden gained believers in a Caliphate (Strengthened the Caliphate).

2. Bin laden firmed up his position as Caliph if a Caliphate came to be (Strengthened his position in the Caliphate's Boss Game).

3. Bin Laden attracted new recruits to Al-Qaeda (Strengthened Al-Qaeda).

4. Bin Laden became the unassailable leader of Al-Qaeda (Strengthened his position in the alliance's Boss Game).

How Bin Laden weakened his enemies on 9/11:

1. Bin Laden created distrust in the Pax Americana (Weakened the Pax Americana).

2. Bin Laden lessened the perception of U.S. strength and leadership of the Pax Americana (Weakened the U.S. position in the Pax Americana's Boss Game).

3. Bin Laden sowed distrust in the alliance between Arab Rulers and the United States (Weakened the U.S.-Arab Alliance).

4. Bin Laden caused allies to doubt U.S. leadership of the U.S.-Arab Alliance (Weakened the U.S. position in the alliance's Boss Game).

The effects of 9/11 looked like this, following the gray arrows:

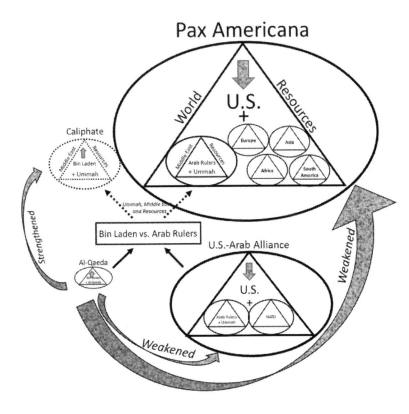

For Bin Laden's strategy, the attacks on 9/11 were tragically effective.

But afterward, what happened?

For ten years, Bin Laden was holed up in Afghanistan,

then Pakistan. Ten years of inactivity, frustrated operations and tactical failures.

And then, Bin Laden was killed on May 2nd, 2011.

Ten years in which Bin Laden didn't strike again.

Why didn't Bin Laden do more while he was alive?

Why didn't Bin Laden attack shopping malls or stadiums or other soft targets?

Did Bin Laden lose the capability or the will to attack?

Or both?

8

Your Strategy

"If you know others and know yourself, you will not be imperiled in a hundred battles." - Sun Tzu[20]

I knocked on my boss's door.

She waved me in. It was a mid-sized office with brown, durable furniture placed at right angles. I sat on a chair with muted stains. She swiveled toward me.

"I know what happened," she said. "But tell me your version."

I started at the beginning.

He was a volunteer, I said. We had several meetings. I tried to put him on a team. We discovered he couldn't keep a secret. And he lied about it, too. Over and over.

"What do you think we should do?" she asked.

End it, I said. It's over.

She nodded. "How will you do it?"

It's tricky, I said. He suspects it's over. But he's probably hoping for a reprieve. He might go on the offensive. Or he might not. Even if he doesn't, he's going to react when I tell him it's over. I'll do it by phone, so he can't do anything stupid. He's done enough stupid things already.

She shook her head. "No, it should be face-to-face. Tell him in no uncertain terms it's over. Make sure there's no doubt he's fired."

A surprise.

A surprise because it was a bad idea. She was telling me to take a risk for no reward.

But I liked this boss. I respected her. So my first thought was I missed something. I thought she saw something I didn't.

I played it through in my head again. How he would react. What he would do when he heard me say it was over.

He would react. No doubt that he would react.

In training, we had a lecturer talk to us about

situations like this. About firing a source. About how to do it by the book. After the lecture, we did an exercise where we did it in role play. We fired an instructor who was acting like a source.

It was an easy exercise. No disguise. No surveillance detection. No weapons. No concealment. Not even an alias.

The instructor assigned to play my source was a nice guy. He didn't pull stunts, like some instructors did. I was glad it was him. Easy in, easy out.

We met in a mock hotel room. I fired him the way the lecturer said to do it. Said everything the lecturer said to say. By the book.

The instructor/source pushed back.

I stuck to what the lecturer had said. I told him exactly what the lecturer had said to say.

There was a pause.

He stood up. He filled his lungs and started screaming. Mostly in a language I didn't know.

He looked like he was going to swing at me. But he swung at a lamp instead. A real lamp, not a mock lamp. The bulb shattered. Broken glass skittered across the floor.

I tried to calm him down.

No luck.

The screaming went on. When in English, it was about his sick child and his poor grandmother and the orphans who lived down the street.

Finally, he stormed out. He slammed the door and yelled all the way down the hall.

I stared at the shattered bulb.

In CIA training, mistakes are not good. Mistakes mean a "less than satisfactory" – a "Lester" - on your record. Enough Lesters, and you're out.

I made a mistake. But I wasn't sure what mistake. I did exactly what the lecturer said. I did it by the book.

The phone rang. It was the instructor.

He said not to worry. He wasn't going to give me a Lester. Because I did what the lecturer said to do.

But what I did was wrong. I didn't see it from the source's side. I didn't anticipate what the source would do. I wasn't ready. I hadn't prepared for what he would do. I had put myself at risk for nothing.

Since then, I'd done real firings. Where I'd done what the instructor, not the lecturer, had said.

Since then, I'd anticipated what the source would do. And planned. And built the right strategy.

And now my boss wanted me to ignore all that. She wanted me to ignore the source's reaction. Ignore that he would already suspect something bad would happen. She wanted me to ignore that the source was thinking of worst-case scenarios.

I wouldn't hurt him. I wouldn't do anything to his family.

But he didn't know that.

Which was a problem.

A strategic problem.

Because he might decide to strike first.

After all, he was a tough guy. Professionally.

Which I knew. And he knew, too.

Dangerous.

And my boss wanted me to do it face-to-face.

Decisions matter when they're acted on. Thinking matters when it's turned into action.

When it's just you, turning decisions into action is easy. You decide what to do and act. Easy.

When you're part of a group, it's more difficult. More difficult because it's usually different people deciding and acting. There's a hierarchy. One person decides, and another person acts on the decision. Which means the people acting have a choice.

The people acting have a veto. The people acting can refuse to act.

Sometimes, people don't know they have a veto. Sometimes, the thought of vetoing a decision has been beaten out of them.[21] Sometimes, a veto is threatened with death.[22]

When you join a group, you accept its hierarchy. If your job is to act on other people's decisions, you do it. You do what the hierarchy tells you to do. You can't veto the decision by not acting. Unless you don't want to be part of the group.

But sometimes groups have different hierarchies for different decisions. One type of decision is made by one hierarchy. A second type of decision is made by a different hierarchy.

Which is what happens in spy organizations.

There's an official hierarchy. And an operational hierarchy.

The official hierarchy decides on personnel, strategic initiatives and resources. The official hierarchy decides which case officers to hire. Where to place them. Who to promote into management.

The operational hierarchy decides on operational issues. Which sources to trust. How to work with them. Which moment-by-moment risks make sense.

At the top of the official hierarchy is who you would think it would be: the agency director.

At the top of the operational hierarchy are the guys on the street: the case officers.

Different hierarchies for different decisions.

Different hierarchies for organizational decisions and operational decisions.[23]

Sometimes, there's a conflict.

When there's a conflict, the operational hierarchy usually wins. But the operational hierarchy doesn't win because the rules say so. The operational hierarchy wins because people in the official hierarchy believe the decisions of case officers should be respected. After all, case officers are the ones at risk.

The operational hierarchy usually wins because people in the official hierarchy respect and admire case officers.

When a case officer needs something, the official hierarchy stops what they're doing. For a case officer, the official hierarchy will stop all activity. They'll stop making personnel decisions. They'll stop advancing strategic initiatives. They'll stop deciding resource allocation issues. They'll stop everything to support the guys on the street.

A few months after being overseas, I stopped by a Headquarters office to talk about a tricky case. It had been a last-minute trip. No time to set up an appointment.

The cubicles were empty. The staff was packed in a conference room. The door was ajar. At the end of a long table, a woman was talking. I asked a man inside the door how long the meeting would last.

The woman at the end of the long table heard me. Annoyed at the interruption, she asked what I wanted.

Now I recognized her. She was twenty years older and eight levels higher. Chief of the CIA's operations for a

---

region of the world.

I apologized for interrupting. I said who I was. What I wanted.

A hush fell over the room.

"You're a case officer?" she asked.

I nodded.

She stood up. "We're done here, everyone." She pointed at three people. "You, you and you: Go help him, immediately."

To me she said, "If they can't help you, let me know. I'll make sure you get it."

I experienced it once with the Director of the CIA himself. After a briefing, he pulled me aside. Turned away from his aides. Away from my boss. Away from my boss's boss. Away from my boss's boss's boss.

He put his arm around me like politicians do. Pulled me close.

He whispered: "You know I'd trade jobs with you, if I could."

I chuckled. Laughed like it was a joke.

"I'm not joking," he said.

Awkward moment. It seemed like he wanted a response.

No thank you, sir, I said.

He laughed loudly. Slapped me on the shoulder. "I don't blame you." He went back to his aides. And my boss. And my boss's boss. And my boss's boss's boss. Who came over and wanted to know what he said.

I shrugged. He wants my job, I told them.

Which he didn't. Not really. Just for a moment after hearing what I was doing, he wanted to be making different decisions. Not personnel and resource decisions. Not political decisions. Not organizational decisions. He wanted to make operational decisions.

Usually, the two hierarchies work well together.

But sometimes, there's a conflict.

Sometimes, the official hierarchy makes a bad decision. Sometimes, they tell a case officer to do something he shouldn't.

At those times, it's risky for the case officer. Because the operational decision-making hierarchy is informal. The personnel and strategic initiative and resource allocation hierarchy is official. In official vs. informal, official usually wins. After all, official is the one on paper.

It's a risk they don't tell you about when you sign up to be a spy. They tell you about the physical risk of working with dangerous people in dangerous places. They make sure you know you could die. They show you the stars on the wall representing people killed in the line of duty. Which you accept when you take the job. It's what you signed up for.

But they don't tell you about the bureaucratic risk. They don't tell you there's the risk that someone in the official hierarchy will disagree with your operational decisions. And punish you for it. After all, the official hierarchy makes decisions about personnel assignments and strategic initiatives and resources. Lots of ways they can punish you.

That was the risk I faced now. A bureaucratic risk.

My boss wanted me to do something I shouldn't.

I looked forward. And reasoned backward.

I knew I had a veto. And I knew most people in the organization would back me up. I knew I could refuse to act on her decision. But I didn't want to do that. I didn't want to use my veto, if I didn't need to.

I didn't want to start a Boss Game. I didn't want to

start a fight over who decided what.

Mostly because I had better things to do.

Instead of being in my boss's office, I should have been on the street. I should have been running sources. And recruiting new ones.

One new source I was working to recruit would be able to target financiers of terrorism.

Terrorism isn't expensive, but it costs something. There are plane tickets. Living expenses. Plus the cost of bombs. And weapons. Which terrorists buy from criminals. Who don't sell anything cheaply. Which means terrorists need money.

One way to stop terrorism is to take away the money. Take away the money for bomb-making equipment and you take away the bomb. Take away the money for plane tickets and living expenses and you take away the terrorists.

That was one tactic after 9/11: Turn off the world banking system to terrorists. Large transfers were flagged. Suspected terrorists got scrutiny.

Which meant terrorists went underground. Cash in suitcases. And low weight, high value items like diamonds. Family exchange networks moved cash, too. To keep it hidden, they made terrorist transfers look like legitimate business transactions.

The source I wanted to recruit had a way to spot some transfers. When I told him what we needed, he liked the idea. He liked the Pax Americana. He wanted a safer world.

But he said no.

It was too risky. He had a wife, he said. He didn't want to put her in danger.

Which made sense.

Terrorists are dangerous people. To be helpful, he would meet terrorists. Which would put his wife at risk.

But he didn't give me a hard no. It was more a "I wish I could, but I can't" kind of no.

Which made sense.

He was in his Endgame.

He had his wife. He had a good income. Plus a nice house in a safe place. Why put that at risk?

When you're in your Endgame, why leave it?

Most people won't. Most people never do. If someone is in their Endgame, they don't want to leave it.

Unless there's a threat.

Not just any threat. An existential threat. A threat to the most important part of any Endgame: its people.

When the people in your Endgame are threatened, your mindset shifts. You see conflict is unavoidable. A fight is coming.

You get ready for war.

You build a strategy. You reason backward. From the Zero-Sum Game back to the Positive-Sum Games that help you win. You reason backward from the conflict to the alliances that will help you win it.

Seven weeks after he said no, a bomb went off.

The bomb went off in his wife's hometown. People died. Horrifically. Some of them, his wife knew. For them, it was like 9/11.

He called me. Wanted to know if my offer was still good. Wanted to know how soon we could meet. How fast he could start.

He was in.

A threat to his Endgame had appeared.

A fight was coming.

It was time to join an alliance with me.

Not everyone likes the Pax Americana. In fact, a lot of people don't.

There were even some in the U.S. Government and CIA who don't like the Pax Americana. Some were quasi-isolationists. They believed the American Endgame stopped at the U.S. border. Others wanted a different Endgame. Others didn't care about the Pax Americana at all. They just wanted a paycheck.

But for most of us, the Pax Americana was our castle. It was what we protected. We'd die for the people in it, if necessary. But we hoped it wouldn't come to that.

One way to protect your castle is to identify threats while they're small and distant. Before they grow into big threats. You want to stop enemies before they're strong enough to threaten you.

So you lay tripwires. You watch for precursors. You look for indicators of what's to come.

Not just on capability. Also on will.

You watch for when someone's capability to attack and their will to attack overlap. You watch for when they become a threat:

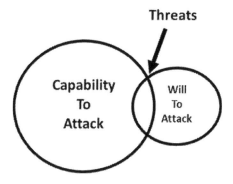

Although we missed it with Bin Laden, capabilities are usually easier to spot. They're usually in the form of weapons. Or soldiers. Or technology.

The will to attack is usually more difficult to spot. But just as important. Maybe, more important. Because if someone has the will to attack you, they'll work hard to get the capability to attack you.

Which means you look around for people with the will

to attack you. You look around for the people who believe the Pax Americana has someone, someplace or something that they need for their Endgame.

You look for people who want either:

1. The people in the Pax Americana, or

2. The places where the Pax Americana exists, or

3. The things that sustain the Pax Americana

Someone who wants those things has the will to attack.

If they're not our enemy already, they'll be our enemy someday.

Which you know. So you watch them. But you need to know what to watch for. So you build hypotheses about what they'll do.

You build hypotheses by reasoning backward through their strategy. From their Endgame to their conflict with you to the alliances they will build. To the alliances they are already building.

You watch for certain alliances and agreements and meetings.

You watch for certain new capacities or trade deals or technology acquisition.

And when you see it, you know what it means.

A confusing world is shrunk to a manageable size.

A size where you can understand others' strategies. Where you can understand when they're preparing to threaten you. And when they're not.

Which means you can choose which threats to take seriously. You can focus on enemies who have the will and capabilities and alliances to threaten you. And you can ignore those who don't.

Which is useful.

If you use it.

When you're a spy, you think a lot about death. You think a lot about the people who died doing what you're doing.

You think about the guy who was shot and no one knows why. You think about the guy who died in a car accident that maybe wasn't an accident. You think about Mike Spann killed in Afghanistan. You think about the people who became stars on the wall at

Headquarters.

You think about death, and you want your death to count. You don't fear it, but you want to make it a good one. You don't want to sell your life cheaply.

You don't want a stupid death. Which means you don't do stupid things. Like go to meetings with tough guy sources who do stupid things.

Rather than fight my boss, I tried to persuade her.

I used math. Then logic. Then reasoned backward.

The best outcome of another meeting was zero, I told her. Because the lying source would react. He might attack. Which I would need to respond to. Which would be a negative. The best we could hope for was zero.

Then there was the logic of first strikes. He might not wait for bad news. He might think it's coming. He might decide he should strike first.

Finally, the big picture. She knew I was working against many different enemies. In many parts of the world.

She knew my work was on a field that looked like this:

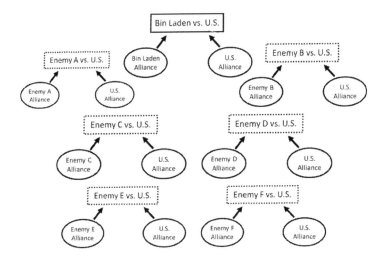

One real conflict: The one against Bin Laden. And a lot of potential conflicts. Which meant infiltrating a lot of potential enemies' alliances.

Reasoning backward, the lying source wasn't even on the field. He was a minor player far from the main conflict. He could have been more of a player, eventually. But he made bad choices. Stupid choices. He was still far from any potential conflict.

It was a dispassionate argument. Mathematical. Logical. Reasonable.

She didn't care.

For her, there was only one thing that mattered: The official hierarchy. She was supposed to tell me what to do. And I was supposed to do it.

But she didn't want to give me an order, if she didn't have to. She wanted to be nice.

So she tried to persuade me.

She said I should do it her way because it's "the way we do things."

An identity argument. A "who we are" argument. A "don't you want to be like the rest of us" argument. An "In-Group" argument.

Stronger than my logical argument.

I felt its pull.

It was persuasive. I didn't want to be part of the Out-Group. Not over one decision. Did I?

I imagined the Endgame again. I reasoned backward.

I said, It still doesn't make sense. I know the guy. I know how he thinks. He's going to do something. Probably, something stupid.

She flushed. Took a breath like she was going to yell, but didn't. She didn't stand up. Didn't walk it off, like some would.

She sat there. Tiny tremors in her face. She wasn't going to back down.

Me neither.

Which meant conflict. A Zero-Sum Game.

But not the worst kind of Zero-Sum Game. Not the one where the loser is vanquished. And not the second worst kind where the conflict goes on and on. At least, I hoped it wouldn't be that kind of game.

I hoped it would be the third type of Zero-Sum Game.

A Boss Game. A Zero-Sum Game over who makes a decision.

One of us would make the decision in this case. The other wouldn't.

One of us would win. One of us would lose.

After it was over, our Positive-Sum Game would continue, I hoped. We'd go back to a win-win relationship.

Which meant I would hold back. Hopefully, she would, too.

She held back by offering something new.

The tremors on her face stopped. She took a deep

breath.

She proposed putting more people on the scene. As protection.

I didn't expect that. I usually worked alone.

But it was generous of her to offer, so I considered it.

More people create a sense of power. In you. And a sense of fear in the other side.

Which is good sometimes. When you're trying to impress somebody, more people help. But more people don't guarantee safety. Sometimes, more people mean more victims.

This guy wasn't a suicide bomber. Too narcissistic for that. But he didn't have to bring a bomb. Or a gun. He could do plenty of damage with his hands. And he might be desperate.

More people could make him panic. Panic can make someone do stupid things. Stupid things with more people around to be victims.

I shook my head.

Adding people made this small game bigger. Big enough that it risked affecting more important games.

The right move was to make this small game smaller.

Contain it. Shrink it. Minimize it to zero. Best option: Get past it quickly.

I said no again. I said more people was a bad idea. More people didn't lower the risk. More people increased it.

She stared at me.

She still wanted to be the decision-maker. She still wanted to win.

She wasn't going to back down.

I sighed and went tactical.

The first step: Call her bluff.

When you're a spy, you're around dangerous people. They're dangerous because they have guns. They have bombs. They have the capability to hurt you. To harm you. To kill you, if they want to.

But usually they don't.

Usually they don't kill you because they don't want to. They could, if they wanted. But they don't want to, so they don't.

They have the capability to attack you, but they don't have the will.

They're here:

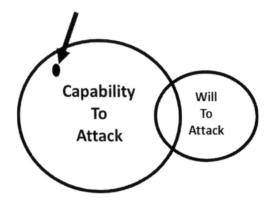

There are two things needed to attack:

1. Capability, and

2. Will.

The more important is always will.

When you look at Bin Laden after 9/11, you see his capabilities were degraded. U.S. forces, allied forces and even non-allied forces worked to take away Bin Laden's capabilities. Hundreds of thousands of people worked billions of hours.

But Bin Laden's capabilities weren't at zero. He could have done something. He could have launched some attack somewhere using somebody. After all, he had ten years. A lot can happen in ten years. But Bin Laden did nothing.

If Bin Laden had the capability to attack but didn't, that means he didn't want to. He didn't have the will.

Which seems strange. Bin Laden had attacked once. His attack had a devastating effect. His attack advanced his strategy in four ways. And weakened his enemies in four ways. Why not attack again?

The answer lies in Bin Laden's strategy.

Bin Laden's Endgame was a Caliphate. Which meant his strategy was built to get the people, places and things for the Caliphate to exist. He wanted the Ummah. He wanted the Middle East. He wanted the resources in the Middle East. Plus, he wanted to be boss of it all. He wanted to be Caliph.

To get there, Bin Laden wanted to separate the U.S. from the Arab Rulers of the Middle East. He wanted to separate the Middle East from the Pax Americana.

Bin Laden wanted this:

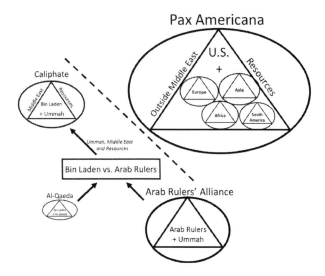

Bin Laden wanted to do things that advanced him on that path. He wanted to do things that got him to his Endgame.

He wanted to do things that increased the chance he would be Caliph.

And he wanted to avoid doing things that would lower the chance of being Caliph. He wanted to make sure few others would compete with him to be Caliph.

If Bin Laden was successful in separating the Pax Americana from the Middle East, a lot of people would want to be Caliph. After every revolution, there's a battle to see who becomes leader. It's not always the revolutionaries who become the rulers. Generals don't always become kings.

Others would want to be Caliph. Others would try to convince the Ummah that they were the true Caliph. That Bin Laden shouldn't be Caliph.

Which Bin Laden wanted to avoid. He wanted to make it so no one else could possibly be Caliph. Bin Laden wanted to be the undisputed, unanimous choice for Caliph, if the Caliphate came to be.

One tactic Bin Laden used for this has been used by potential kings throughout history: Do extraordinary things.

Bin Laden didn't do ordinary things. He didn't do the kinds of attacks that others could do.

Bin Laden launched grandiose attacks. Bin Laden did extraordinary things.

It's not a new tactic for kings. Or wannabe kings.

It's why there are kingly legends. If you're a king, you tell everyone you did something extraordinary. Maybe you tell everyone you did something superhuman, like pulling a sword from a stone. If people believe it, rivals will have a hard time toppling you. Because rivals would need to build an alliance to topple you. And any of their potential allies would ask, "Did you do an extraordinary thing?"

The attacks on 9/11 were an extraordinary thing. They took a lot of preparation. A lot of planning. A lot of resources. They took someone who could bring it all together. They took a mastermind.[24]

The attacks on 9/11 advanced Bin Laden's strategy in four important ways. Maybe most important for Bin Laden was that he became the undisputed choice for Caliph by doing an extraordinary thing.

Bin Laden didn't want to lose what he had gained. He didn't want to lose his leadership position. He didn't want to lose his spot at the top of the Caliphate, if the Caliphate came to be.

Bin Laden didn't want to do ordinary things.

Bin Laden didn't want to do things that any competitors for Caliph could do. That they could take on as their own.

After 9/11, the worry of many Americans was that Bin Laden would do suicide bombings against soft targets. Against shopping malls, stadiums and parks.

But suicide bombings like that aren't extraordinary things. They don't take a lot of preparation, planning or resources. They only require a bombmaker and somebody willing to blow themselves up. Which is why suicide bombings are frequent in some parts of the world. They don't take a mastermind.

Suicide bombings like that are relatively easy to do. Which is why a lot of Americans feared them after 9/11.

But Bin Laden had reason to fear them, too.

If suicide bombings became prevalent in the United States, could Bin Laden claim credit? Or would someone else? Could Bin Laden keep control of them? Or would others in the movement become leaders? Would Bin Laden lose what he had gained?

After 9/11, Bin Laden was the undisputed leader of his movement. Undisputed leader of Al-Qaeda. If a Caliphate came to be, Bin Laden was first in line to be Caliph.

If random suicide bombings became the favored tactic of jihadis, it wasn't clear that Bin Laden would stay in control.

After all, Bin Laden was pinned down in Afghanistan and Pakistan. Others could take the lead.

I don't know if Bin Laden ever said no to a suicide attack on a shopping mall in the United States. But it would have been a tactic that went against his strategy. It would have opened him up to competition for Caliph. Competition Bin Laden didn't want.

Not that Bin Laden wouldn't attack the United States again. He would, if he could. But he wanted his next attack to be an extraordinary thing.

Bin Laden wanted his next attack to be something that advanced his strategy the way 9/11 had. He wanted to do an extraordinary thing to make the Caliphate more likely. An extraordinary thing to separate the United States from Arab allies.

Bin Laden wanted to do something extraordinary. Something grandiose.

Like detonating a nuclear weapon in the United States.

Detonating a nuclear weapon in the United States fit Bin Laden's strategy. It would have done the eight things that 9/11 did for his strategy. Maybe more.

If Bin Laden got a nuclear weapon, he would have used it. Which is why a lot of people worked very hard to be sure Bin Laden never got a nuclear weapon. A lot of people on the other side of Bin Laden's strategy.

The thing about strategy is that the other side has a strategy, too. The other side has an Endgame. And a Boss Game in it. The other side looks forward. The other side reasons backward through Zero-Sum Games and Positive-Sum Games. And back to today.

The other side always has a strategy.

For Bin Laden, the other side was the United States. And we had a strategy.

We had an Endgame. And a Boss Game in it.

We had the Pax Americana and our homeland to protect.

We reasoned backward to the Zero-Sum Game Bin Laden wanted to play against us. To the Positive-Sum alliances we needed to win.

Bin Laden had his strategy. We had ours.

We had a strategy.

Worse for Bin Laden, we had the tactical capability to carry it out.

The Pax Americana was weakened on 9/11. Everybody felt it.

Plus, the U.S.-Arab alliance was weakened. Distrust damaged its foundation.

Which meant we had problems. We had a lot of rebuilding to do.

But we also wanted to go on the attack. We wanted to make sure something like 9/11 never happened again.

Our strategy for Bin Laden looked like this:

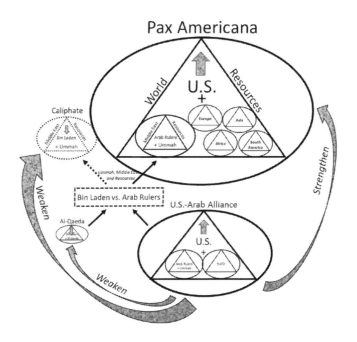

After 9/11, the strategy was to weaken four things:

1. Al-Qaeda.

2. Bin Laden's leadership of Al-Qaeda.

3. The possibility of a Caliphate.

4. Bin Laden's standing as future leader of a Caliphate.

At the same time, the strategy was to strengthen:

1. The Pax Americana.

2. U.S. leadership of the Pax Americana.

3. The U.S.-Arab Alliance

4. The U.S. position in the U.S.-Arab Alliance.

The U.S. strategy was Bin Laden's strategy in reverse.

The U.S. was on the same playing field as Bin Laden. With opposite purposes.

We wanted to strengthen where Bin Laden wanted to weaken. We wanted to weaken where Bin Laden wanted to strengthen.

Which we did. Over ten years. Ten years of little steps. Little tactical steps.

Tactical steps aimed at weakening Bin Laden.

Tactical steps aimed at strengthening ourselves.

Most of which are classified.[25]

Then came May 2011.

Bin Laden was in our sights.

It didn't matter whether U.S. operatives had Pakistani permission to take Bin Laden family DNA. It didn't matter whether Saudi Arabia or any other ally approved. It didn't matter whether U.S. Forces had Pakistani permission to enter their air space.

On May 2nd, 2011, the U.S. didn't consult with allies. Didn't even tell them what happened until it was over.

On that day, U.S. Special Operators killed Bin Laden.

Never would Bin Laden be Caliph. Never would his vision come to be.

Bin Laden's strategy was over.

But Bin Laden wasn't the only one who wanted a Caliphate.

Others wanted the Ummah under their control. Others wanted the land and resources of the Middle East. Others wanted to pull the Middle East out of the Pax Americana.

Others wanted a Caliphate.

For them, Bin Laden's body could become a rallying point. His grave could become a shrine.

So Bin Laden's body was flown to sea. It was dropped in the deep. So it could never be a rallying point. So his grave could never be a shrine.

Next, ISIS would rise. Another group who wanted a Caliphate.

Its leaders would build a strategy to get it. A different strategy from Bin Laden's. Based on their own capabilities. And will. They wanted to pull the Middle East out of the Pax Americana.

But ISIS wasn't the only threat to the Pax Americana.

Others wanted the people in the Pax Americana. Or the places. Or the things in the Pax Americana. Others had Endgames that conflicted with the Pax Americana.

Which you watch for, when you're a spy. You watch for people acquiring the capability to attack you. You watch for people acquiring certain technology and weapons. You watch for people building alliances to attack you.

But more than that, you watch for other people's Endgames. You watch for who has the will to attack you.

When you identify Endgames that conflict with yours, you reason backward. Like they are. To the alliances they're building. To when they're preparing to attack you.

You watch for others who have the capabilities and will to attack you.

You watch for threats.

If you're good at it, you see threats before they hit you. You see the enemy's plans before they attack.

Which means your side has the advantage. Your side can disrupt the enemy's alliance. Your side can attack pre-emptively. Your side can remove an enemy's capability before it's used. Which saves a lot of lives.

To do that, you take risks. You go to tricky places. You do dangerous things.

It's risky.

But you don't do dumb things.

You don't put yourself in situations where there's nothing to gain and a lot to lose. You don't play Zero-Sum Games where your best result is zero.

Because when a Zero-Sum Game begins, strategy goes out the window.

Your DADA cycle shrinks. You and the other side react in real time.

No more theory. No more strategy. Just reality.

And reality always brings a surprise. There's always something you didn't anticipate. You might look for a knife or gun and get head-butted. There's always something you didn't count on. There's always an unexpected risk.

Which means you choose the games you play carefully.

You choose games where the reward is worth the risk.

You choose games you'll win.

I called my boss's bluff.

I told my boss we should go see her boss. The Chief. We should let the Chief decide whose decision would win.

Which meant neither of us would be the decision-maker.

The Chief would be the decision-maker.

My boss wasn't happy about it. But I was respecting the official hierarchy. Which meant she couldn't disagree.

When we went to see the Chief, the Chief wasn't there. Her assistant made an appointment for the next day.

Another night to think about my arguments for the Chief. But I had already thought enough about this case. I was ready to be done with it. So I didn't think about it anymore.

My boss did. She had thought about it more. When we saw the Chief the next day, my boss had another new idea.

We started in plush chairs. Another government-inspired color scheme. But bigger. Glittery awards on the walls. Famous people in photos.

My boss told the story. Most of it. Not all of it. Not as much context as I would have. But enough. Then she said she told me to have another meeting. And I said no.

The Chief asked me what the problem was.

Another meeting was the wrong thing to do, I said.

"Why?" she asked.

This time I didn't walk through the math, reason or logic.

I focused on the guy. I said he'd probably do something stupid. Why give him a chance?

The Chief frowned. Turned to my boss. The Chief said

what I expected her to say. What almost everyone in her position would say.

"Why don't we do what he wants to do?" she asked.

My boss ignored the question. Said she had another idea.

"Let's set up a meeting and observe him from a distance. We'll see his frame of mind. See if he's agitated."

A surprise.

The Chief turned to me. "What do you think?"

I thought there were two possible results:

1. He shows up agitated.

2. Or he doesn't.

Either way, it meant nothing. Because he could be calm and planning something stupid. Or he could get agitated later and do something stupid.

Either way, it meant nothing.

But it was good bureaucratic move. My boss could delay losing our little conflict. Plus it allowed my boss to save face. It allowed her to re-assert her position. It avoided a Boss Game. Which I was happy to avoid, too.

And her gambit wasted resources. A hallmark of bureaucratic strategies.

I wasn't happy because it meant more time away from important things. A waste. But I couldn't say no. Which was why my boss proposed it.

So I said ok.

My boss was happy.

The Chief was happy.

After wasting some resources, I would be happy.

I set up the meeting. Observed him. He was calm, not agitated. Which meant nothing.

I went to tell my boss. She pretended to be busy. For a couple days. Another delaying tactic.

Then, she left town. So I did what she wanted me to do: I skipped over her.

I went to the Chief and got the okay.

I went to a payphone. A payphone picked at random.

Some years later, that payphone would be in the blast radius of a suicide bomber. It was ripped apart by ball bearings.

But not that day. That day there was no suicide

———————————————

bomber. That day there was just me picking up the phone and making a call.

The lying source answered on the fifth ring.

He said he was out of town. Whether he was lying or not, it didn't matter. Not anymore.

I told him it was over.

His throat caught. His voice shook. He had a reaction.

He had known it was coming. But now it was real. So he had the reaction. The reaction to loss. The reaction that makes your adrenaline surge. The reaction that makes you do stupid things. If stupid things are possible.

Stupid things weren't possible. At least, not directed at me. Because I was at a random payphone. And he was somewhere else.

He choked out, "Ok."

I thanked him again. Wished him good luck.

Again a choked out, "Ok."

I hung up.

I walked away.

Maybe I should have gone to the meeting. Maybe

nothing would have happened. Maybe I should have done what my boss said. Maybe I should have taken the risk.

Or maybe I should have gone in ready for a fight.

Maybe I should have started something. Maybe I should have thrown a punch. Maybe I should have struck first. Maybe I should have been a tough guy.

But that wouldn't have been a spy's strategy.

A spy's strategy starts with an Endgame. A spy's strategy means reasoning backward. Reasoning backward through the interactions. It means playing the games that get you to the Endgame. In a way that protects the people, places and things in your Endgame.

A spy's strategy means you give up opportunities for shootouts. It means you hold your punches. It means you bypass bloodshed unless there's no other option. And if there's no other option, you made a mistake.

It's rare you start conflicts. It's rare you fight.

Unless there is a Zero-Sum Game between you and your Endgame.

After the lying source, I played many more important games. More Positive-Sum Games. But, not all were Positive-Sum Games.

Some were Zero-Sum Games.

Some were the third type of Zero-Sum Game. Conflicts over who decides what.

Some were the second type of Zero-Sum Game. Conflicts over people, places and things again and again.

Some were the first type of Zero-Sum Game. Conflicts where the loser is vanquished. Never seen again.

But all were more important than the game with the lying source.

One of those more important games was with you.

By the time you read this, the Pax Americana may be gone. Maybe something else has replaced it. Maybe something better. Probably something worse.

Maybe you want something different. Maybe you want an Endgame built with the same people, places and things but under different rules. With someone else as boss.

Maybe, you want to be boss.

If so, you'll need to understand three things about strategy:

1. You can't have a strategy without an Endgame. If world domination is your Endgame, your Endgame will conflict with lots of other people's Endgames. And being boss of that Endgame will conflict with lots of other people's ambitions. Which means you'll have to reason backward through a lot of Zero-Sum Games.

2. To win those Zero-Sum Games, you'll need to play Positive-Sum Games. You'll need lots of mutually-beneficial alliances.

3. Inside your Positive-Sum Games will be Boss Games. Especially inside your alliances. Somebody will make the most important decisions. You want that person to be you. So you can decide how to win the Zero-Sum Games. So you can be boss of your Endgame.

Strategy is looking forward and reasoning backward. Backward through the Positive-Sum and Zero-Sum Games you'll need to play. All the way back to today.

Strategy is imagination and reason.

But building a strategy isn't the end.

In getting things done, building a strategy is not even the midway point. It's almost the beginning.

After you've imagined the Endgame and reasoned backward, you'll go forward.

You'll act.

It looks like this:

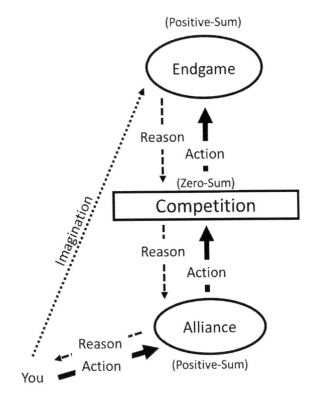

Success requires three things:

1. Imagining an Endgame.

2. Reasoning backward through the games you'll play.

3. Taking action.

Most people are good at imagination. Or reasoning backward. Or action. Or maybe two of the three.

But few are good at all three.

It's hard to be good at all three. It's hard to be good at imagination, reason and action.

Which is why few strategies are successful.

Which is why few people reach their Endgame.

Plus, there are people on the other side. People with their own Endgames in mind. People who may start a conflict with you. People who want what you have. Or who will resist giving you what you want. People who may join your alliance for a time, then betray you. People who have their own strategies to pursue.

This book is the Endgame of a strategy. A small strategy. A micro-strategy. But a strategy all the same.

To get here, I imagined a Positive-Sum Game with you. I imagined you reading it. But you aren't just anyone. I imagined you were somebody interested in strategy. Or wanted to know more about spies. Or about how spies think about strategy.

From there, I reasoned backward. Backward through the Zero-Sum Game of competition.

This book had a lot of competition. There are millions, maybe billions, of other books you could read.

To win that Zero-Sum Game, this book needed an alliance. It needed a marketing service. An artist. A book distributor. If you're reading this in a language other than English, it needed a translator. All of whom needed to gain from their effort. It needed to be a Positive-Sum Game.

That was the strategy.

Then, it was time to act. It was time to write. It was time to build those alliances with a marketing service, artist and book distributor. If you're reading this in a language other than English, it was time to build an alliance with a translator, too.

It looked like this:

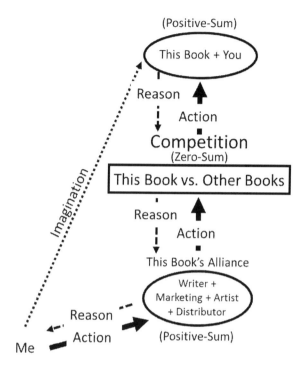

The action took much longer than the imagining and reasoning. Much longer. As action usually does.

Then the book was done.

It competed and won your attention. It beat out the other books.

This book became a place where a Positive-Sum Game

took place. Between me and you. At least, if you enjoyed it. If you got something out of it.

If so, the strategy and tactics worked.

We both got to the Endgame of this micro-strategy.

Now, our game is over.

Unless you buy another of my books.

If you liked *A Spy's Guide to Thinking + Strategy*, a review at Amazon would be a generous thing for you to do:

https://www.amazon.com/B074DZQZBY

You can also join the Spy's Guide email newsletter to hear about upcoming books, blog posts, and events at:

https://spysguide.com

When you join, you'll get updates on new books, blog posts on spy's guide topics and occasional surprises.

You can follow John on Twitter at:

twitter.com/spysguide

Thank you for reading!

[1] In this discussion of games, I'm leaning on game theory terminology but not using it exactly the way a game theorist would. For example: the term "Positive-Sum" (rarely used by game theorists – they prefer "non Zero-Sum"). Strictly speaking, game theorists could use "Positive-Sum" to refer to an interaction where one side's gain supersedes the other's, even if the other side loses. Here, I'm using "Positive-Sum" to refer to interactions where both sides win. This is also the way it's come to be used in popular culture. Probably because it's more useful for thinking.

[2] There are two other types of outcomes: If one of us thought a fight was coming, but the other didn't, it would probably come. If neither thought a fight was coming, then it wouldn't. Payoffs are like in a Prisoner's Dilemma.

[3] An ANGLICO Marine, specifically. He was a member of the elite "Air Naval Gunfire Liaison Company."

[4] Dixit and Nalebuff, *Thinking Strategically*.

[5] Which they never did, as far as I know.

[6] To give the airport screeners the benefit of the doubt, the fact that I had the residue of so many types of explosives on

my shoes made it look more like a false positive than a real threat. If someone is making a bomb, they are more likely to have only one or two types of explosives residue on their shoes, not every type known to man.

☐ As before, this term is used in a different way from how some game theorists would use it. In fact, most wouldn't use the term "Positive-Sum" at all. They prefer "non-Zero-Sum." Here, "Positive-Sum" refers to interactions where both sides win. This is also the way it's come to be used in popular culture. Probably because it's more useful for thinking and strategy.

8 These are sometimes called Cooperative (Positive-Sum) and Competitive (Zero-Sum) games. But those words imply certain points on the range of Positive-Sum and Zero-Sum Games. Which is why we're using the broader terms Positive-Sum and Zero-Sum. The Positive-Sum/Zero-Sum distinction leaves out things as all models do. But you gain more than you lose, as you'll see.

9 Otherwise known as "nouns."

10 Italy was there, too, but they were far weaker than the other "major" powers.

11 Which is partly why Germany attacked first in August 1914. If you think a war is coming and you feel weak, you look for another way to even the odds. Like a surprise attack.

12 To learn more, read anything on the "Venona Transcripts."

13 In the political science world, it's said this is the event that transitioned the Soviet Union from being an "ideological

state" to a "traditional state."

14 It's a separate story how Chambers became so disillusioned that he stopped being a Communist.

15 Sometimes, people think an Endgame doesn't need to be a Positive-Sum Game because they're using bad analogies. Since most bad analogies come from the movies, they're probably thinking of characters like Conan the Barbarian. He's motivated by revenge, to satisfy himself or to do his duty to his ancestors (a Positive-Sum Game in his mind). Or you might be thinking of Keyser Soze from the *Usual Suspects*, who killed his family rather than lose to his enemies. But movie characters are bad analogies because Keyser Soze and Conan only exist in movies created for a Positive-Sum Game between the filmmaker(s) and the audience.

16 After the Soviet-Afghan War, there would be a civil war to determine *which* Afghans would rule. But after the Soviets withdrew in 1989, Endgame A existed, such as it was.

17 The "one thing" has such a history that spy movie and thriller screenwriters have a name for the thing a spy is seeking or protecting: A "MacGuffin."

18 This would also include situations where the loser continues to lose game after game. Like slavery, where the loser is perpetually having things taken (their labor) involuntarily and gaining nothing in return.

19 Some presidents make this transition earlier than others because they previously served in high positions, such George H.W. Bush. Sometimes, events like 9/11 force the shift. But you never see the shift in the opposite direction. You never

see Presidents start off doing things internationally, then go back to focus on domestic issues.

[20] That statement is sometimes translated as "If you know your enemies," but that's wrong. The literal translation is: "If you know others." Which means it applies to enemies and allies and everyone else. In other words, the other side of both Zero-Sum Games and Positive-Sum Games.

[21] This is one of the purposes of bootcamp. Maybe, the main purpose.

[22] Which is why soldiers who don't follow orders on the frontlines are shot.

[23] Originally, it was this way due to the slow speed of communications. People at the headquarters had no way of getting all the data needed in time to make a good operational decision, so the operational decision was left to people in the field. With a higher speed of communication, this may change.

[24] Khalid Sheikh Mohammed is often called the "mastermind of 9/11," but he worked for Bin Laden.

[25] Tactical steps are usually classified, but strategies rarely are. The vision and the reasoning backward are usually open to the public. But tactical actions and capabilities are kept secret. To preserve the element of surprise.

Printed in Great Britain
by Amazon